LUKE + ACTS

A MESSAGE OF RESCUE

Bible Society
Trinity Business Centre
Stonehill Green, Westlea
Swindon SN5 7DG
biblesociety.org.uk

Cover design by Big Blond Bear
Cover photograph by Stephen Arnold, unsplash.com
All internal images from unsplash.com

Typesetting and production by Bible Society Resources Ltd, a wholly
owned subsidiary of The British and Foreign Bible Society

ISBN: 978-0-56-405337-7

BSRL/3M/2021

Printed in Great Britain

Luke+Acts: A Message of Rescue

Welcome to *Luke+Acts: A Message of Rescue*. This book is an action-packed account of the life of Jesus and his diverse band of followers, taken directly from two books of the Bible, the Gospel of Luke and the book of Acts.

What is a Gospel?

The word 'gospel' literally means 'good news' and refers to the overall Christian message of the Bible – God's saving acts for us through Jesus' teachings, his death and resurrection and the coming of the kingdom of God.

Early in the history of Christianity, the word 'gospel' came to be used to refer to the books of the New Testament that tell the story of Jesus' life, death and resurrection – the books in which this message of good news is told. The four books accepted by most Christians as Gospels are Matthew, Mark, Luke and John. Each of these Gospels offers a different account and understanding of Jesus and his divine role. They were written by different people and for different audiences – but they are one story of good news.

Luke and Acts

The Gospel according to Luke and the book of Acts are traditionally said to have been written by a doctor called Luke who lived in the Greek city of Antioch, in modern-day Turkey. Luke makes it clear at the beginning of his Gospel that he wasn't a direct witness of Jesus' life but did extensive research to ensure his account was accurate. He was a follower of the apostle Paul and is likely to have been an eyewitness to at least some of the events described in the book of Acts. However, in both books, Luke is keen not just to describe what happened but also to explain why it matters.

In traditional Christian art, each of the Gospel writers is represented by a symbol. This symbolism started appearing around 100 years after Jesus' death, but is commonly associated with St Jerome, a translator of the Bible, in the fourth century, and was expanded by a monk, Rabanus Maurus, around AD 800.

Luke is represented by an ox or bull, a symbol of both strength and sacrifice (because these animals were often used in ritual sacrifice). His Gospel is focused on what happened to Jesus and why, with an emphasis on Jesus' strength and sacrifice on the cross, which forms a central part of God's rescue plan for creation.

It's also suggested that each symbol has a further meaning – that it reflects a quality or virtue that Christians should show in the way they live. In the case of the ox or bull, it's believed that this signifies the importance of our own strength and the call to sacrifice ourselves by following Jesus.

A message of rescue

The core part of Luke's account in his Gospel and the book of Acts is his exploration of the theme of salvation, of how God will rescue us. Luke explores this by looking at how God has acted to save us in the past (by referencing the Old Testament), how he acted in Jesus' life, death and resurrection, and how he will continue to act in the future.

Throughout the following pages, you will find ten reflections based on this theme of God's rescue of us, framed by our human journey in the Bible of creation, fall and salvation.

We hope that this book – the story of Jesus' birth, life and death and God's mission of rescue that we're all invited to join – starts you on a deeper journey with the Bible.

[1] Dear Theophilus:

Many people have done their best to write a report of the things that have taken place among us. [2] They wrote what we have been told by those who saw these things from the beginning and who proclaimed the message. [3] And so, your Excellency, because I have carefully studied all these matters from their beginning, I thought it would be good to write an orderly account for you. [4] I do this so that you will know the full truth about everything which you have been taught.

The Birth of John the Baptist is Announced

[5] During the time when Herod was king of Judea, there was a priest named Zechariah, who belonged to the priestly order of Abijah. His wife's name was Elizabeth; she also belonged to a priestly family. [6] They both lived good lives in God's sight and obeyed fully all the Lord's laws and commands. [7] They had no children because Elizabeth could not have any, and she and Zechariah were both very old.

[8] One day Zechariah was doing his work as a priest in the Temple, taking his turn in the daily service. [9] According to the custom followed by the priests, he was chosen by lot to burn incense on the altar. So he went into the Temple of the Lord, [10] while the crowd of people outside prayed during the hour when the incense was burnt.

[11] An angel of the Lord appeared to him, standing on the right of the altar where the incense was burnt. [12] When Zechariah saw him, he was alarmed and felt afraid. [13] But the angel said to him, "Don't be afraid, Zechariah! God has heard your prayer, and your wife Elizabeth will bear you a son. You are to name him John. [14] How glad and happy you will be, and how happy many others will be when he is born! [15] He will be a great man in the Lord's sight. He must not drink any wine or strong drink. From his very birth he will be filled with the Holy Spirit, [16] and he will bring back many of the people of Israel to the Lord their God. [17] He will go ahead of the Lord, strong and mighty like the prophet Elijah. He will bring fathers and children together again; he will turn disobedient people back to the way of thinking of the righteous; he will get the Lord's people ready for him."

[18] Zechariah said to the angel, "How shall I know if this is so? I am an old man, and my wife is old also."

[19] "I am Gabriel," the angel answered. "I stand in the presence of God, who sent me to speak to you and tell you this good news. [20] But you have not believed my message, which will come true at the right time.

Because you have not believed, you will be unable to speak; you will remain silent until the day my promise to you comes true."

²¹ In the meantime the people were waiting for Zechariah and wondering why he was spending such a long time in the Temple. ²² When he came out, he could not speak to them, and so they knew that he had seen a vision in the Temple. Unable to say a word, he made signs to them with his hands.

²³ When his period of service in the Temple was over, Zechariah went back home. ²⁴ Some time later his wife Elizabeth became pregnant and did not leave the house for five months. ²⁵ "Now at last the Lord has helped me," she said. "He has taken away my public disgrace!"

The Birth of Jesus is Announced

²⁶ In the sixth month of Elizabeth's pregnancy God sent the angel Gabriel to a town in Galilee named Nazareth. ²⁷ He had a message for a young woman promised in marriage to a man named Joseph, who was a descendant of King David. Her name was Mary. ²⁸ The angel came to her and said, "Peace be with you! The Lord is with you and has greatly blessed you!"

²⁹ Mary was deeply troubled by the angel's message, and she wondered what his words meant. ³⁰ The angel said to her, "Don't be afraid, Mary; God has been gracious to you. ³¹ You will become pregnant and give birth to a son, and you will name him Jesus. ³² He will be great and will be called the Son of the Most High God. The Lord God will make him a king, as his ancestor David was, ³³ and he will be the king of the descendants of Jacob for ever; his kingdom will never end!"

³⁴ Mary said to the angel, "I am a virgin. How, then, can this be?"

³⁵ The angel answered, "The Holy Spirit will come on you, and God's power will rest upon you. For this reason the holy child will be called the Son of God. ³⁶ Remember your relative Elizabeth. It is said that she cannot have children, but she herself is now six months pregnant, even though she is very old. ³⁷ For there is nothing that God cannot do."

³⁸ "I am the Lord's servant," said Mary; "may it happen to me as you have said." And the angel left her.

Mary Visits Elizabeth

³⁹ Soon afterwards Mary got ready and hurried off to a town in the hill country of Judea. ⁴⁰ She went into Zechariah's house and greeted

Elizabeth. [41] When Elizabeth heard Mary's greeting, the baby moved within her. Elizabeth was filled with the Holy Spirit [42] and said in a loud voice, "You are the most blessed of all women, and blessed is the child you will bear! [43] Why should this great thing happen to me, that my Lord's mother comes to visit me? [44] For as soon as I heard your greeting, the baby within me jumped with gladness. [45] How happy you are to believe that the Lord's message to you will come true!"

Mary's Song of Praise

[46] Mary said,

> "My heart praises the Lord;
> [47]   my soul is glad because of God my Saviour,
> [48]   for he has remembered me, his lowly servant!
> From now on all people will call me happy,
> [49]   because of the great things the Mighty God has done for
>   me.
> His name is holy;
> [50]   from one generation to another
> he shows mercy to those who honour him.
> [51] He has stretched out his mighty arm
> and scattered the proud with all their plans.
> [52] He has brought down mighty kings from their thrones,
> and lifted up the lowly.
> [53] He has filled the hungry with good things,
> and sent the rich away with empty hands.
> [54] He has kept the promise he made to our ancestors,
> and has come to the help of his servant Israel.
> [55] He has remembered to show mercy to Abraham
> and to all his descendants for ever!"

[56] Mary stayed about three months with Elizabeth and then went back home.

The Birth of John the Baptist

[57] The time came for Elizabeth to have her baby, and she gave birth to a son. [58] Her neighbours and relatives heard how wonderfully good the Lord had been to her, and they all rejoiced with her.

[59] When the baby was a week old, they came to circumcise him, and they were going to name him Zechariah, after his father. [60] But his mother said, "No! His name is to be John."

[61] They said to her, "But you have no relatives with that name!" [62] Then they made signs to his father, asking him what name he would like the boy to have.

[63] Zechariah asked for a writing tablet and wrote, "His name is John." How surprised they all were! [64] At that moment Zechariah was able to speak again, and he started praising God. [65] The neighbours were all filled with fear, and the news about these things spread through all the hill country of Judea. [66] Everyone who heard of it thought about it and asked, "What is this child going to be?" For it was plain that the Lord's power was upon him.

Zechariah's Prophecy

[67] John's father Zechariah was filled with the Holy Spirit, and he spoke God's message:

[68] "Let us praise the Lord, the God of Israel!
    He has come to the help of his people and has set them free.
[69] He has provided for us a mighty Saviour,
    a descendant of his servant David.
[70] He promised through his holy prophets long ago
[71]   that he would save us from our enemies,
    from the power of all those who hate us.
[72] He said he would show mercy to our ancestors
    and remember his sacred covenant.
[73-74] With a solemn oath to our ancestor Abraham
    he promised to rescue us from our enemies
    and allow us to serve him without fear,
[75] so that we might be holy and righteous before him
    all the days of our life.

[76] "You, my child, will be called a prophet of the Most High God.
    You will go ahead of the Lord to prepare his road for him,
[77] to tell his people that they will be saved
    by having their sins forgiven.
[78] Our God is merciful and tender.
    He will cause the bright dawn of salvation to rise on us
[79]   and to shine from heaven on all those who live in the dark shadow of death,
    to guide our steps into the path of peace."

[80] The child grew and developed in body and spirit. He lived in the desert until the day when he appeared publicly to the people of Israel.

The Birth of Jesus

[1] At that time the Emperor Augustus ordered a census to be taken throughout the Roman Empire. [2] When this first census took place, Quirinius was the governor of Syria. [3] Everyone, then, went to register himself, each to his own town.

[4] Joseph went from the town of Nazareth in Galilee to the town of Bethlehem in Judea, the birthplace of King David. Joseph went there because he was a descendant of David. [5] He went to register with Mary, who was promised in marriage to him. She was pregnant, [6] and while they were in Bethlehem, the time came for her to have her baby. [7] She gave birth to her first son, wrapped him in strips of cloth and laid him in a manger — there was no room for them to stay in the inn.

The Shepherds and the Angels

[8] There were some shepherds in that part of the country who were spending the night in the fields, taking care of their flocks. [9] An angel of the Lord appeared to them, and the glory of the Lord shone over them. They were terribly afraid, [10] but the angel said to them, "Don't be afraid! I am here with good news for you, which will bring great joy to all the people. [11] This very day in David's town your Saviour was born — Christ the Lord! [12] And this is what will prove it to you: you will find a baby wrapped in strips of cloth and lying in a manger."

[13] Suddenly a great army of heaven's angels appeared with the angel, singing praises to God:

> [14] "Glory to God in the highest heaven,
>   and peace on earth to those with
>   whom he is pleased!"

[15] When the angels went away from them back into heaven, the shepherds said to one another, "Let's go to Bethlehem and see this thing that has happened, which the Lord has told us."

[16] So they hurried off and found Mary and Joseph and saw the baby lying in the manger. [17] When the shepherds saw him, they told them what the angel had said about the child. [18] All who heard it were amazed at what the shepherds said. [19] Mary remembered all these things and thought deeply about them. [20] The shepherds went back, singing praises to God for all they had heard and seen; it had been just as the angel had told them.

Jesus is Named

21 A week later, when the time came for the baby to be circumcised, he was named Jesus, the name which the angel had given him before he had been conceived.

Jesus is Presented in the Temple

22 The time came for Joseph and Mary to perform the ceremony of purification, as the Law of Moses commanded. So they took the child to Jerusalem to present him to the Lord, 23 as it is written in the law of the Lord: "Every firstborn male is to be dedicated to the Lord." 24 They also went to offer a sacrifice of a pair of doves or two young pigeons, as required by the law of the Lord.

25 At that time there was a man named Simeon living in Jerusalem. He was a good, God-fearing man and was waiting for Israel to be saved. The Holy Spirit was with him 26 and had assured him that he would not die before he had seen the Lord's promised Messiah. 27 Led by the Spirit, Simeon went into the Temple. When the parents brought the child Jesus into the Temple to do for him what the Law required, 28 Simeon took the child in his arms and gave thanks to God:

29 "Now, Lord, you have kept your promise,
    and you may let your servant go in peace.
30 With my own eyes I have seen your salvation,
31   which you have prepared
        in the presence of all peoples:
32 A light to reveal your will to the Gentiles
    and bring glory to your people Israel."

33 The child's father and mother were amazed at the things Simeon said about him. 34 Simeon blessed them and said to Mary, his mother, "This child is chosen by God for the destruction and the salvation of many in Israel. He will be a sign from God which many people will speak against 35 and so reveal their secret thoughts. And sorrow, like a sharp sword, will break your own heart."

36-37 There was a very old prophet, a widow named Anna, daughter of Phanuel of the tribe of Asher. She had been married for only seven years and was now 84 years old. She never left the Temple; day and night she worshipped God, fasting and praying. 38 That very same hour she arrived and gave thanks to God and spoke about the child to all who were waiting for God to set Jerusalem free.

The Return to Nazareth

[39] When Joseph and Mary had finished doing all that was required by the law of the Lord, they returned to their home town of Nazareth in Galilee. [40] The child grew and became strong; he was full of wisdom, and God's blessings were upon him.

The Boy Jesus in the Temple

[41] Every year the parents of Jesus went to Jerusalem for the Passover Festival. [42] When Jesus was twelve years old, they went to the festival as usual. [43] When the festival was over, they started back home, but the boy Jesus stayed in Jerusalem. His parents did not know this; [44] they thought that he was with the group, so they travelled a whole day and then started looking for him among their relatives and friends. [45] They did not find him, so they went back to Jerusalem looking for him. [46] On the third day they found him in the Temple, sitting with the Jewish teachers, listening to them and asking questions. [47] All who heard him were amazed at his intelligent answers. [48] His parents were astonished when they saw him, and his mother said to him, "My son, why have you done this to us? Your father and I have been terribly worried trying to find you."

[49] He answered them, "Why did you have to look for me? Didn't you know that I had to be in my Father's house?" [50] But they did not understand his answer.

[51] So Jesus went back with them to Nazareth, where he was obedient to them. His mother treasured all these things in her heart. [52] Jesus grew both in body and in wisdom, gaining favour with God and people.

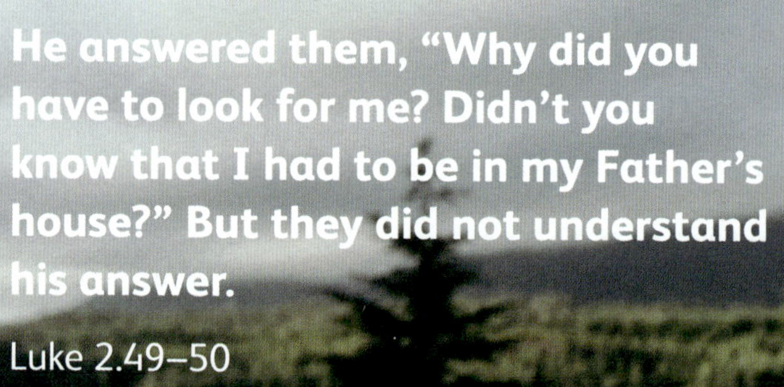

He answered them, "Why did you have to look for me? Didn't you know that I had to be in my Father's house?" But they did not understand his answer.

Luke 2.49–50

Reflect

Zechariah, Elizabeth, Mary, Simeon and Anna all recognise the beginning of something special with the arrival of Jesus, but sometimes in life we can become so focused on little things that we forget the big things. Twelve years after Simeon's incredible prophecy that, through Jesus, God had kept his promise to save all people (page 10), Jesus' parents seem to have slipped into the routine of looking after him like any other child.

But even as a young boy Jesus understands who he is and his relationship with God. He is surprised that his parents wonder where he would be, because for him it's obvious – he's exactly where he should be. It's important that these are the first recorded words of Jesus in Luke's Gospel; it's his opening statement – I know who I am, and I know why I'm here.

We don't always have that same certainty that Jesus had. We get bogged down by the day-to-day of life and we can start to lose focus, producing an uncertainty that can make life harder to deal with – an uncertainty that could even see us drift down the wrong path. In Jesus, we can find some sense of the path we should be on and start to see the signs of God's activity in our lives – where we're from, and who we really are. That belonging can bring a peace greater than anything else.

Pray

Lord, my creator,
cut through the noise of the day-to-day
and keep me focused on the important things:
that you made me
and that you love me.
Guide me on the right path:
a path of certainty,
a path of love,
a path of peace.
Amen

Act

In the noise of life, can you find five minutes of quiet every day
to listen? Doing activities like gardening, reading, or exercise
might offer you a peaceful place to shut out the noise around
you and listen. What do you feel? What do you hear?

The Preaching of John the Baptist

[1] It was the fifteenth year of the rule of the Emperor Tiberius; Pontius Pilate was governor of Judea, Herod was ruler of Galilee, and his brother Philip was ruler of the territory of Iturea and Trachonitis; Lysanias was ruler of Abilene, [2] and Annas and Caiaphas were high priests. At that time the word of God came to John son of Zechariah in the desert. [3] So John went throughout the whole territory of the River Jordan, preaching, "Turn away from your sins and be baptized, and God will forgive your sins."

[4] As it is written in the book of the prophet Isaiah:
"Someone is shouting in the desert:
    'Get the road ready for the Lord;
    make a straight path for him to travel!
[5] Every valley must be filled up,
    every hill and mountain levelled off.
The winding roads must be made straight,
    and the rough paths made smooth.
[6] The whole human race will see God's salvation!' "

[7] Crowds of people came out to John to be baptized by him. "You snakes!" he said to them. "Who told you that you could escape from the punishment God is about to send? [8] Do those things that will show that you have turned from your sins. And don't start saying among yourselves that Abraham is your ancestor. I tell you that God can take these stones and make descendants for Abraham! [9] The axe is ready to cut down the trees at the roots; every tree that does not bear good fruit will be cut down and thrown in the fire."

[10] The people asked him, "What are we to do, then?"

[11] He answered, "Whoever has two shirts must give one to the man who has none, and whoever has food must share it."

[12] Some tax collectors came to be baptized, and they asked him, "Teacher, what are we to do?"

[13] "Don't collect more than is legal," he told them.

[14] Some soldiers also asked him, "What about us? What are we to do?"

He said to them, "Don't take money from anyone by force or accuse anyone falsely. Be content with your pay."

[15] People's hopes began to rise, and they began to wonder whether John perhaps might be the Messiah. [16] So John said to all of them,

"I baptize you with water, but someone is coming who is much greater than I am. I am not good enough even to untie his sandals. He will baptize you with the Holy Spirit and fire. [17]He has his winnowing shovel with him, to thresh out all the grain and gather the wheat into his barn; but he will burn the chaff in a fire that never goes out."

[18]In many different ways John preached the Good News to the people and urged them to change their ways. [19]But John reprimanded Herod, the governor, because he had married Herodias, his brother's wife, and had done many other evil things. [20]Then Herod did an even worse thing by putting John in prison.

The Baptism of Jesus

[21]After all the people had been baptized, Jesus also was baptized. While he was praying, heaven was opened, [22]and the Holy Spirit came down upon him in bodily form like a dove. And a voice came from heaven, "You are my own dear Son. I am pleased with you."

The Ancestors of Jesus

[23]When Jesus began his work, he was about thirty years old. He was the son, so people thought, of Joseph, who was the son of Heli, [24]the son of Matthat, the son of Levi, the son of Melchi, the son of Jannai, the son of Joseph, [25]the son of Mattathias, the son of Amos, the son of Nahum, the son of Esli, the son of Naggai, [26]the son of Maath, the son of Mattathias, the son of Semein, the son of Josech, the son of Joda, [27]the son of Joanan, the son of Rhesa, the son of Zerubbabel, the son of Shealtiel, the son of Neri, [28]the son of Melchi, the son of Addi, the son of Cosam, the son of Elmadam, the son of Er, [29]the son of Joshua, the son of Eliezer, the son of Jorim, the son of Matthat, the son of Levi, [30]the son of Simeon, the son of Judah, the son of Joseph, the son of Jonam, the son of Eliakim, [31]the son of Melea, the son of Menna, the son of Mattatha, the son of Nathan, the son of David, [32]the son of Jesse, the son of Obed, the son of Boaz, the son of Salmon, the son of Nahshon, [33]the son of Amminadab, the son of Admin, the son of Arni, the son of Hezron, the son of Perez, the son of Judah, [34]the son of Jacob, the son of Isaac, the son of Abraham, the son of Terah, the son of Nahor, [35]the son of Serug, the son of Reu, the son of Peleg, the son of Eber, the son of Shelah, [36]the son of Cainan, the son of Arphaxad, the son of Shem, the son of Noah, the son of Lamech, [37]the son of Methuselah, the son of Enoch, the son of Jared, the son of Mahalaleel, the son of Kenan, [38]the son of Enosh, the son of Seth, the son of Adam, the son of God.

The Temptation of Jesus

[1] Jesus returned from the Jordan full of the Holy Spirit and was led by the Spirit into the desert, [2] where he was tempted by the Devil for forty days. In all that time he ate nothing, so that he was hungry when it was over.

[3] The Devil said to him, "If you are God's Son, order this stone to turn into bread."

[4] But Jesus answered, "The scripture says, 'Human beings cannot live on bread alone.'"

[5] Then the Devil took him up and showed him in a second all the kingdoms of the world. [6] "I will give you all this power and all this wealth," the Devil told him. "It has all been handed over to me, and I can give it to anyone I choose. [7] All this will be yours, then, if you worship me."

[8] Jesus answered, "The scripture says, 'Worship the Lord your God and serve only him!'"

[9] Then the Devil took him to Jerusalem and set him on the highest point of the Temple, and said to him, "If you are God's Son, throw yourself down from here. [10] For the scripture says, 'God will order his angels to take good care of you.' [11] It also says, 'They will hold you up with their hands so that not even your feet will be hurt on the stones.'"

[12] But Jesus answered, "The scripture says, 'Do not put the Lord your God to the test.'"

[13] When the Devil finished tempting Jesus in every way, he left him for a while.

Jesus Begins his Work in Galilee

[14] Then Jesus returned to Galilee, and the power of the Holy Spirit was with him. The news about him spread throughout all that territory. [15] He taught in the synagogues and was praised by everyone.

Jesus is Rejected at Nazareth

[16] Then Jesus went to Nazareth, where he had been brought up, and on the Sabbath he went as usual to the synagogue. He stood up to read the Scriptures [17] and was handed the book of the prophet Isaiah. He unrolled the scroll and found the place where it is written:

[18] "The Spirit of the Lord is upon me,
    because he has chosen me to bring good news to the poor.

> He has sent me to proclaim liberty to the captives
>   and recovery of sight to the blind;
>   to set free the oppressed
> 19   and announce that the time has come
>   when the Lord will save his people."

20 Jesus rolled up the scroll, gave it back to the attendant, and sat down. All the people in the synagogue had their eyes fixed on him, 21 as he said to them, "This passage of scripture has come true today, as you heard it being read."

22 They were all well impressed with him and marvelled at the eloquent words that he spoke. They said, "Isn't he the son of Joseph?"

23 He said to them, "I am sure that you will quote this proverb to me, 'Doctor, heal yourself.' You will also tell me to do here in my home town the same things you heard were done in Capernaum. 24 I tell you this," Jesus added, "prophets are never welcomed in their home town.

25 "Listen to me: it is true that there were many widows in Israel during the time of Elijah, when there was no rain for 3.5 years and a severe famine spread throughout the whole land. 26 Yet Elijah was not sent to anyone in Israel, but only to a widow living in Zarephath in the territory of Sidon. 27 And there were many people suffering from a dreaded skin disease who lived in Israel during the time of the prophet Elisha; yet not one of them was healed, but only Naaman the Syrian."

28 When the people in the synagogue heard this, they were filled with anger. 29 They rose up, dragged Jesus out of the town, and took him to the top of the hill on which their town was built. They meant to throw him over the cliff, 30 but he walked through the middle of the crowd and went his way.

A Man with an Evil Spirit

31 Then Jesus went to Capernaum, a town in Galilee, where he taught the people on the Sabbath. 32 They were all amazed at the way he taught, because he spoke with authority. 33 In the synagogue was a man who had the spirit of an evil demon in him; he screamed out in a loud voice, 34 "Ah! What do you want with us, Jesus of Nazareth? Are you here to destroy us? I know who you are: you are God's holy messenger!"

35 Jesus ordered the spirit, "Be quiet and come out of the man!" The demon threw the man down in front of them and went out of him without doing him any harm.

[36] The people were all amazed and said to one another, "What kind of words are these? With authority and power this man gives orders to the evil spirits, and they come out!" [37] And the report about Jesus spread everywhere in that region.

Jesus Heals Many People

[38] Jesus left the synagogue and went to Simon's house. Simon's mother-in-law was sick with a high fever, and they spoke to Jesus about her. [39] He went and stood at her bedside and ordered the fever to leave her. The fever left her, and she got up at once and began to wait on them.

[40] After sunset all who had friends who were sick with various diseases brought them to Jesus; he placed his hands on every one of them and healed them all. [41] Demons also went out from many people, screaming, "You are the Son of God!"

Jesus gave the demons an order and would not let them speak, because they knew that he was the Messiah.

Jesus Preaches in the Synagogues

[42] At daybreak Jesus left the town and went off to a lonely place. The people started looking for him, and when they found him, they tried to keep him from leaving. [43] But he said to them, "I must preach the Good News about the Kingdom of God in other towns also, because that is what God sent me to do."

[44] So he preached in the synagogues throughout the country.

Jesus Calls the First Disciples

¹One day Jesus was standing on the shore of Lake Gennesaret while the people pushed their way up to him to listen to the word of God. ²He saw two boats pulled up on the beach; the fishermen had left them and were washing the nets. ³Jesus got into one of the boats — it belonged to Simon — and asked him to push off a little from the shore. Jesus sat in the boat and taught the crowd.

⁴When he finished speaking, he said to Simon, "Push the boat out further to the deep water, and you and your partners let down your nets for a catch."

⁵"Master," Simon answered, "we worked hard all night long and caught nothing. But if you say so, I will let down the nets." ⁶They let them down and caught such a large number of fish that the nets were about to break. ⁷So they motioned to their partners in the other boat to come and help them. They came and filled both boats so full of fish that the boats were about to sink. ⁸When Simon Peter saw what had happened, he fell on his knees before Jesus and said, "Go away from me, Lord! I am a sinful man!"

⁹He and the others with him were all amazed at the large number of fish they had caught. ¹⁰The same was true of Simon's partners, James and John, the sons of Zebedee. Jesus said to Simon, "Don't be afraid; from now on you will be catching people."

¹¹They pulled the boats up on the beach, left everything, and followed Jesus.

Jesus Heals a Man

¹²Once Jesus was in a town where there was a man who was suffering from a dreaded skin disease. When he saw Jesus, he threw himself down and begged him, "Sir, if you want to, you can make me clean!"

¹³Jesus stretched out his hand and touched him. "I do want to," he answered. "Be clean!" At once the disease left the man. ¹⁴Jesus ordered him, "Don't tell anyone, but go straight to the priest and let him examine you; then to prove to everyone that you are cured, offer the sacrifice as Moses ordered."

¹⁵But the news about Jesus spread all the more widely, and crowds of people came to hear him and be healed from their diseases. ¹⁶But he would go away to lonely places, where he prayed.

Jesus Heals a Paralysed Man

[17] One day when Jesus was teaching, some Pharisees and teachers of the Law were sitting there who had come from every town in Galilee and Judea and from Jerusalem. The power of the Lord was present for Jesus to heal the sick. [18] Some men came carrying a paralysed man on a bed, and they tried to take him into the house and put him in front of Jesus. [19] Because of the crowd, however, they could find no way to take him in. So they carried him up on the roof, made an opening in the tiles, and let him down on his bed into the middle of the group in front of Jesus. [20] When Jesus saw how much faith they had, he said to the man, "Your sins are forgiven, my friend."

[21] The teachers of the Law and the Pharisees began to say to themselves, "Who is this man who speaks such blasphemy! God is the only one who can forgive sins!"

[22] Jesus knew their thoughts and said to them, "Why do you think such things? [23] Is it easier to say, 'Your sins are forgiven you,' or to say, 'Get up and walk'? [24] I will prove to you, then, that the Son of Man has authority on earth to forgive sins." So he said to the paralysed man, "I tell you, get up, pick up your bed, and go home!"

[25] At once the man got up in front of them all, took the bed he had been lying on, and went home, praising God. [26] They were all completely amazed! Full of fear, they praised God, saying, "What marvellous things we have seen today!"

Jesus Calls Levi

[27] After this, Jesus went out and saw a tax collector named Levi, sitting in his office. Jesus said to him, "Follow me." [28] Levi got up, left everything, and followed him.

[29] Then Levi had a big feast in his house for Jesus, and among the guests was a large number of tax collectors and other people. [30] Some Pharisees and some teachers of the Law who belonged to their group complained to Jesus' disciples. "Why do you eat and drink with tax collectors and other outcasts?" they asked.

[31] Jesus answered them, "People who are well do not need a doctor, but only those who are sick. [32] I have not come to call respectable people to repent, but outcasts."

The Question about Fasting

33 Some people said to Jesus, "The disciples of John fast frequently and offer prayers, and the disciples of the Pharisees do the same; but your disciples eat and drink."

34 Jesus answered, "Do you think you can make the guests at a wedding party go without food as long as the bridegroom is with them? Of course not! 35 But the day will come when the bridegroom will be taken away from them, and then they will fast."

36 Jesus also told them this parable: "No one tears a piece off a new coat to patch up an old coat. If he does, he will have torn the new coat, and the piece of new cloth will not match the old. 37 Nor does anyone pour new wine into used wineskins, because the new wine will burst the skins, the wine will pour out, and the skins will be ruined. 38 Instead, new wine must be poured into fresh wineskins! 39 And no one wants new wine after drinking old wine. 'The old is better,' he says."

Jesus answered them, "People who are well do not need a doctor, but only those who are sick. I have not come to call respectable people to repent, but outcasts."

Luke 5.31–32

Reflect

Jesus chose to spend much of his time with people others would consider outcasts or on the edge of society. Some of these people were so lost to society that they were almost invisible to those around them, because they were looked upon as sinners and wrongdoers, or people felt they had no value. Jesus however shone a light on those society rejected or ignored, because he saw past what they had done and knew they were equally loved by God.

Levi, or Matthew as he is called in versions of this story in other Gospels, is a tax collector. In first-century Palestine tax collectors were hated because the taxes they collected were for the Romans – they were seen as helping the enemy. But here was Jesus eating and drinking with them. This particular tax collector went on to become a major follower of Jesus, and may even have been the man who wrote Matthew's Gospel. Far from being lost, Levi would go on to be central to Jesus' mission. The religious leaders Jesus is talking to thought they were right, but in truth they were simply self-righteous because they lacked the most important thing – love.

For Jesus no one is lost, no one is excluded. We are all welcome. Jesus came to find and heal those society viewed as lost. He responds quickly to our invitation to be found.

Pray

Jesus, finder of the lost,
guide me and heal me.
Shine a light on every part of me,
and make whole every area of my life.
Open my eyes to those around me
on whom people have turned their backs,
and let me be a light for them.
Amen

Act

We are as guilty today as people were in Jesus' time of making
outcasts invisible and of making people feel they have no value.
Look around you for people others may have turned their backs
on. What could you do to help them feel valued? Be there for
them, don't judge them but show empathy, and let them know
they are loved.

The Question about the Sabbath

[1] Jesus was walking through some cornfields on the Sabbath. His disciples began to pick the ears of corn, rub them in their hands, and eat the grain. [2] Some Pharisees asked, "Why are you doing what our Law says you cannot do on the Sabbath?"

[3] Jesus answered them, "Haven't you read what David did when he and his men were hungry? [4] He went into the house of God, took the bread offered to God, ate it, and gave it also to his men. Yet it is against our Law for anyone except the priests to eat that bread."

[5] And Jesus concluded, "The Son of Man is Lord of the Sabbath."

The Man with a Paralysed Hand

[6] On another Sabbath Jesus went into a synagogue and taught. A man was there whose right hand was paralysed. [7] Some teachers of the Law and some Pharisees wanted a reason to accuse Jesus of doing wrong, so they watched him closely to see if he would heal on the Sabbath. [8] But Jesus knew their thoughts and said to the man, "Stand up and come here to the front." The man got up and stood there. [9] Then Jesus said to them, "I ask you: what does our Law allow us to do on the Sabbath? To help or to harm? To save someone's life or destroy it?" [10] He looked around at them all; then he said to the man, "Stretch out your hand." He did so, and his hand became well again.

[11] They were filled with rage and began to discuss among themselves what they could do to Jesus.

Jesus Chooses the Twelve Apostles

[12] At that time Jesus went up a hill to pray and spent the whole night there praying to God. [13] When day came, he called his disciples to him and chose twelve of them, whom he named apostles: [14] Simon (whom he named Peter) and his brother Andrew; James and John, Philip and Bartholomew, [15] Matthew and Thomas, James son of Alphaeus, and Simon (who was called the Patriot), [16] Judas son of James, and Judas Iscariot, who became the traitor.

Jesus Teaches and Heals

[17] When Jesus had come down from the hill with the apostles, he stood on a level place with a large number of his disciples. A large crowd of people was there from all over Judea and from Jerusalem and from the coastal cities of Tyre and Sidon; [18] they had come to hear him and

to be healed of their diseases. Those who were troubled by evil spirits also came and were healed. [19] All the people tried to touch him, for power was going out from him and healing them all.

Happiness and Sorrow

[20] Jesus looked at his disciples and said,

> "Happy are you poor;
>   the Kingdom of God is yours!
> [21] Happy are you who are hungry now;
>   you will be filled!
> Happy are you who weep now;
>   you will laugh!

[22] "Happy are you when people hate you, reject you, insult you, and say that you are evil, all because of the Son of Man! [23] Be glad when that happens, and dance for joy, because a great reward is kept for you in heaven. For their ancestors did the very same things to the prophets.

> [24] "But how terrible for you who are rich now;
>   you have had your easy life!
> [25] How terrible for you who are full now;
>   you will go hungry!
> How terrible for you who laugh now;
>   you will mourn and weep!

[26] "How terrible when all people speak well of you; their ancestors said the very same things about the false prophets.

Love for Enemies

[27] "But I tell you who hear me: love your enemies, do good to those who hate you, [28] bless those who curse you, and pray for those who ill-treat you. [29] If anyone hits you on one cheek, let him hit the other one too; if someone takes your coat, let him have your shirt as well. [30] Give to everyone who asks you for something, and when someone takes what is yours, do not ask for it back. [31] Do for others just what you want them to do for you.

[32] "If you love only the people who love you, why should you receive a blessing? Even sinners love those who love them! [33] And if you do good only to those who do good to you, why should you receive a blessing? Even sinners do that! [34] And if you lend only to those from

whom you hope to get it back, why should you receive a blessing? Even sinners lend to sinners, to get back the same amount! [35] No! Love your enemies and do good to them; lend and expect nothing back. You will then have a great reward, and you will be children of the Most High God. For he is good to the ungrateful and the wicked. [36] Be merciful just as your Father is merciful.

Judging Others

[37] "Do not judge others, and God will not judge you; do not condemn others, and God will not condemn you; forgive others, and God will forgive you. [38] Give to others, and God will give to you. Indeed, you will receive a full measure, a generous helping, poured into your hands — all that you can hold. The measure you use for others is the one that God will use for you."

[39] And Jesus told them this parable: "One blind man cannot lead another one; if he does, both will fall into a ditch. [40] No pupil is greater than his teacher; but every pupil, when he has completed his training, will be like his teacher.

[41] "Why do you look at the speck in your brother's eye, but pay no attention to the log in your own eye? [42] How can you say to your brother, 'Please, brother, let me take that speck out of your eye,' yet cannot even see the log in your own eye? You hypocrite! First take the log out of your own eye, and then you will be able to see clearly to take the speck out of your brother's eye.

A Tree and its Fruit

[43] "A healthy tree does not bear bad fruit, nor does a poor tree bear good fruit. [44] Every tree is known by the fruit it bears; you do not pick figs from thorn bushes or gather grapes from bramble bushes. [45] A good person brings good out of the treasure of good things in his heart; a bad person brings bad out of his treasure of bad things. For the mouth speaks what the heart is full of.

The Two House Builders

[46] "Why do you call me, 'Lord, Lord,' and yet don't do what I tell you? [47] Anyone who comes to me and listens to my words and obeys them — I will show you what he is like. [48] He is like a man who, in building his house, dug deep and laid the foundation on rock. The river overflowed and hit that house but could not shake it, because it was well built.

[49] But anyone who hears my words and does not obey them is like a man who built his house without laying a foundation; when the flood hit that house it fell at once — and what a terrible crash that was!"

Jesus Heals a Roman Officer's Servant

[1] When Jesus had finished saying all these things to the people, he went to Capernaum. [2] A Roman officer there had a servant who was very dear to him; the man was sick and about to die. [3] When the officer heard about Jesus, he sent some Jewish elders to ask him to come and heal his servant. [4] They came to Jesus and begged him earnestly, "This man really deserves your help. [5] He loves our people and he himself built a synagogue for us."

[6] So Jesus went with them. He was not far from the house when the officer sent friends to tell him, "Sir, don't trouble yourself. I do not deserve to have you come into my house, [7] neither do I consider myself worthy to come to you in person. Just give the order, and my servant will get well. [8] I, too, am a man placed under the authority of superior officers, and I have soldiers under me. I order this one, 'Go!' and he goes; I order that one, 'Come!' and he comes; and I order my slave, 'Do this!' and he does it."

[9] Jesus was surprised when he heard this; he turned round and said to the crowd following him, "I tell you, I have never found faith like this, not even in Israel!"

[10] The messengers went back to the officer's house and found his servant well.

Jesus Raises a Widow's Son

[11] Soon afterwards Jesus went to a town called Nain, accompanied by his disciples and a large crowd. [12] Just as he arrived at the gate of the town, a funeral procession was coming out. The dead man was the only son of a woman who was a widow, and a large crowd from the town was with her. [13] When the Lord saw her, his heart was filled with pity for her, and he said to her, "Don't cry." [14] Then he walked over and touched the coffin, and the men carrying it stopped. Jesus said, "Young man! Get up, I tell you!" [15] The dead man sat up and began to talk, and Jesus gave him back to his mother.

[16] They all were filled with fear and praised God. "A great prophet has appeared among us!" they said; "God has come to save his people!"

[17] This news about Jesus went out through all the country and the surrounding territory.

The Messengers from John the Baptist

[18] When John's disciples told him about all these things, he called two of them [19] and sent them to the Lord to ask him, "Are you the

one John said was going to come, or should we expect someone else?"

²⁰ When they came to Jesus, they said, "John the Baptist sent us to ask if you are the one he said was going to come, or if we should expect someone else."

²¹ At that very time Jesus cured many people of their sicknesses, diseases, and evil spirits, and gave sight to many blind people. ²² He answered John's messengers, "Go back and tell John what you have seen and heard: the blind can see, the lame can walk, those who suffer from dreaded skin diseases are made clean, the deaf can hear, the dead are raised to life, and the Good News is preached to the poor. ²³ How happy are those who have no doubts about me!"

²⁴ After John's messengers had left, Jesus began to speak about him to the crowds: "When you went out to John in the desert, what did you expect to see? A blade of grass bending in the wind? ²⁵ What did you go out to see? A man dressed up in fancy clothes? People who dress like that and live in luxury are found in palaces! ²⁶ Tell me, what did you go out to see? A prophet? Yes indeed, but you saw much more than a prophet. ²⁷ For John is the one of whom the scripture says: 'God said, I will send my messenger ahead of you to open the way for you.' ²⁸ I tell you," Jesus added, "John is greater than anyone who has ever lived. But the one who is least in the Kingdom of God is greater than John."

²⁹ All the people heard him; they and especially the tax collectors were the ones who had obeyed God's righteous demands and had been baptized by John. ³⁰ But the Pharisees and the teachers of the Law rejected God's purpose for themselves and refused to be baptized by John.

³¹ Jesus continued, "Now to what can I compare the people of this day? What are they like? ³² They are like children sitting in the market place. One group shouts to the other, 'We played wedding music for you, but you wouldn't dance! We sang funeral songs, but you wouldn't cry!' ³³ John the Baptist came, and he fasted and drank no wine, and you said, 'He has a demon in him!' ³⁴ The Son of Man came, and he ate and drank, and you said, 'Look at this man! He is a glutton and a drinker, a friend of tax collectors and other outcasts!' ³⁵ God's wisdom, however, is shown to be true by all who accept it."

Jesus at the Home of Simon the Pharisee

³⁶ A Pharisee invited Jesus to have dinner with him, and Jesus went to his house and sat down to eat. ³⁷ In that town was a woman who lived

a sinful life. She heard that Jesus was eating in the Pharisee's house, so she brought an alabaster jar full of perfume [38] and stood behind Jesus, by his feet, crying and wetting his feet with her tears. Then she dried his feet with her hair, kissed them, and poured the perfume on them. [39] When the Pharisee saw this, he said to himself, "If this man really were a prophet, he would know who this woman is who is touching him; he would know what kind of sinful life she lives!"

[40] Jesus spoke up and said to him, "Simon, I have something to tell you."

"Yes, Teacher," he said, "tell me."

[41] "There were two men who owed money to a moneylender," Jesus began. "One owed him 500 silver coins, and the other owed him fifty. [42] Neither of them could pay him back, so he cancelled the debts of both. Which one, then, will love him more?"

[43] "I suppose," answered Simon, "that it would be the one who was forgiven more."

"You are right," said Jesus. [44] Then he turned to the woman and said to Simon, "Do you see this woman? I came into your home, and you gave me no water for my feet, but she has washed my feet with her tears and dried them with her hair. [45] You did not welcome me with a kiss, but she has not stopped kissing my feet since I came. [46] You provided no olive oil for my head, but she has covered my feet with perfume. [47] I tell you, then, the great love she has shown proves that her many sins have been forgiven. But whoever has been forgiven little shows only a little love."

[48] Then Jesus said to the woman, "Your sins are forgiven."

[49] The others sitting at the table began to say to themselves, "Who is this, who even forgives sins?"

[50] But Jesus said to the woman, "Your faith has saved you; go in peace."

Women who Accompanied Jesus

[1] Some time later Jesus travelled through towns and villages, preaching the Good News about the Kingdom of God. The twelve disciples went with him, [2] and so did some women who had been healed of evil spirits and diseases: Mary (who was called Magdalene), from whom seven demons had been driven out; [3] Joanna, whose husband Chuza was an officer in Herod's court; and Susanna, and many other women who used their own resources to help Jesus and his disciples.

The Parable of the Sower

[4] People kept coming to Jesus from one town after another; and when a great crowd gathered, Jesus told this parable:

[5] "Once there was a man who went out to sow corn. As he scattered the seed in the field, some of it fell along the path, where it was stepped on, and the birds ate it up. [6] Some of it fell on rocky ground, and when the plants sprouted, they dried up because the soil had no moisture. [7] Some of the seed fell among thorn bushes, which grew up with the plants and choked them. [8] And some seeds fell in good soil; the plants grew and produced corn, a hundred each."

And Jesus concluded, "Listen, then, if you have ears!"

The Purpose of the Parables

[9] His disciples asked Jesus what this parable meant, [10] and he answered, "The knowledge of the secrets of the Kingdom of God has been given to you, but to the rest it comes by means of parables, so that they may look but not see, and listen but not understand.

Jesus Explains the Parable of the Sower

[11] "This is what the parable means: the seed is the word of God. [12] The seeds that fell along the path stand for those who hear; but the Devil comes and takes the message away from their hearts in order to keep them from believing and being saved. [13] The seeds that fell on rocky ground stand for those who hear the message and receive it gladly. But it does not sink deep into them; they believe only for a while but when the time of testing comes, they fall away. [14] The seeds that fell among thorn bushes stand for those who hear; but the worries and riches and pleasures of this life crowd in and choke them, and their fruit never ripens. [15] The seeds that fell in good soil stand for those who hear the message and retain it in a good and obedient heart, and they persist until they bear fruit.

A Lamp under a Bowl

[16] "People do not light a lamp and cover it with a bowl or put it under a bed. Instead, they put it on the lampstand, so that people will see the light as they come in.

[17] "Whatever is hidden away will be brought out into the open, and whatever is covered up will be found and brought to light.

[18] "Be careful, then, how you listen; because those who have something will be given more, but those who have nothing will have taken away from them even the little they think they have."

Jesus' Mother and Brothers

[19] Jesus' mother and brothers came to him, but were unable to join him because of the crowd. [20] Someone said to Jesus, "Your mother and brothers are standing outside and want to see you."

[21] Jesus said to them all, "My mother and brothers are those who hear the word of God and obey it."

Jesus Calms a Storm

[22] One day Jesus got into a boat with his disciples and said to them, "Let us go across to the other side of the lake." So they started out. [23] As they were sailing, Jesus fell asleep. Suddenly a strong wind blew down on the lake, and the boat began to fill with water, so that they were all in great danger. [24] The disciples went to Jesus and woke him up, saying, "Master, Master! We are about to die!"

Jesus got up and gave an order to the wind and the stormy water; they died down, and there was a great calm. [25] Then he said to the disciples, "Where is your faith?"

But they were amazed and afraid, and said to one another, "Who is this man? He gives orders to the winds and waves, and they obey him!"

Jesus Heals a Man with Demons

[26] Jesus and his disciples sailed on over to the territory of Gerasa, which is across the lake from Galilee. [27] As Jesus stepped ashore, he was met by a man from the town who had demons in him. For a long time this man had gone without clothes and would not stay at home, but spent his time in the burial caves. [28] When he saw Jesus, he gave a loud cry, threw himself down at his feet, and shouted, "Jesus, Son of the Most High God! What do you want with me? I beg you, don't punish me!"

[29] He said this because Jesus had ordered the evil spirit to go out of him. Many times it had seized him, and even though he was kept a prisoner, his hands and feet fastened with chains, he would break the chains and be driven by the demon out into the desert.

[30] Jesus asked him, "What is your name?"

"My name is 'Mob'," he answered — because many demons had gone into him. [31] The demons begged Jesus not to send them into the abyss.

[32] There was a large herd of pigs near by, feeding on a hillside. So the demons begged Jesus to let them go into the pigs, and he let them. [33] They went out of the man and into the pigs. The whole herd rushed down the side of the cliff into the lake and was drowned.

[34] The men who had been taking care of the pigs saw what happened, so they ran off and spread the news in the town and among the farms. [35] People went out to see what had happened, and when they came to Jesus, they found the man from whom the demons had gone out sitting at the feet of Jesus, clothed and in his right mind; and they were all afraid. [36] Those who had seen it told the people how the man had been cured. [37] Then all the people from that territory asked Jesus to go away, because they were terribly afraid. So Jesus got into the boat and left. [38] The man from whom the demons had gone out begged Jesus, "Let me go with you."

But Jesus sent him away, saying, [39] "Go back home and tell what God has done for you."

The man went through the town, telling what Jesus had done for him.

Jairus' Daughter and the Woman who Touched Jesus' Cloak

[40] When Jesus returned to the other side of the lake, the people welcomed him, because they had all been waiting for him. [41] Then a man named Jairus arrived; he was an official in the local synagogue. He threw himself down at Jesus' feet and begged him to go to his home, [42] because his only daughter, who was twelve years old, was dying.

As Jesus went along, the people were crowding him from every side. [43] Among them was a woman who had suffered from severe bleeding for twelve years; she had spent all she had on doctors, but no one had been able to cure her. [44] She came up in the crowd behind Jesus and touched the edge of his cloak, and her bleeding stopped at once. [45] Jesus asked, "Who touched me?"

Everyone denied it, and Peter said, "Master, the people are all round you and crowding in on you."

⁴⁶ But Jesus said, "Someone touched me, for I knew it when power went out of me." ⁴⁷ The woman saw that she had been found out, so she came trembling and threw herself at Jesus' feet. There in front of everybody, she told him why she had touched him and how she had been healed at once. ⁴⁸ Jesus said to her, "My daughter, your faith has made you well. Go in peace."

⁴⁹ While Jesus was saying this, a messenger came from the official's house. "Your daughter has died," he told Jairus; "don't bother the Teacher any longer."

⁵⁰ But Jesus heard it and said to Jairus, "Don't be afraid; only believe, and she will be well."

⁵¹ When he arrived at the house, he would not let anyone go in with him except Peter, John, and James, and the child's father and mother. ⁵² Everyone there was crying and mourning for the child. Jesus said, "Don't cry; the child is not dead — she is only sleeping!"

⁵³ They all laughed at him, because they knew that she was dead. ⁵⁴ But Jesus took her by the hand and called out, "Get up, my child!" ⁵⁵ Her life returned, and she got up at once, and Jesus ordered them to give her something to eat. ⁵⁶ Her parents were astounded, but Jesus commanded them not to tell anyone what had happened.

Jesus Sends Out the Twelve Disciples

¹ Jesus called the twelve disciples together and gave them power and authority to drive out all demons and to cure diseases. ² Then he sent them out to preach the Kingdom of God and to heal the sick, ³ after saying to them, "Take nothing with you for the journey: no stick, no beggar's bag, no food, no money, not even an extra shirt. ⁴ Wherever you are welcomed, stay in the same house until you leave that town; ⁵ wherever people don't welcome you, leave that town and shake the dust off your feet as a warning to them."

⁶ The disciples left and travelled through all the villages, preaching the Good News and healing people everywhere.

Herod's Confusion

⁷ When Herod, the ruler of Galilee, heard about all the things that were happening, he was very confused, because some people were saying that John the Baptist had come back to life. ⁸ Others were saying that Elijah had appeared, and still others that one of the prophets of long ago had come back to life. ⁹ Herod said, "I had John's head cut off; but who is this man I hear these things about?" And he kept trying to see Jesus.

Jesus Feeds a Great Crowd

¹⁰ The apostles came back and told Jesus everything they had done. He took them with him, and they went off by themselves to a town called Bethsaida. ¹¹ When the crowds heard about it, they followed him. He welcomed them, spoke to them about the Kingdom of God, and healed those who needed it.

¹² When the sun was beginning to set, the twelve disciples came to him and said, "Send the people away so that they can go to the villages and farms round here and find food and lodging, because this is a lonely place."

¹³ But Jesus said to them, "You yourselves give them something to eat."

They answered, "All we have are five loaves and two fish. Do you want us to go and buy food for this whole crowd?" ¹⁴ (There were about 5,000 men there.)

Jesus said to his disciples, "Make the people sit down in groups of about fifty each."

¹⁵ After the disciples had done so, ¹⁶ Jesus took the five loaves and two fish, looked up to heaven, thanked God for them, broke them, and

gave them to the disciples to distribute to the people. [17] They all ate and had enough, and the disciples took up twelve baskets of what was left over.

Peter's Declaration about Jesus

[18] One day when Jesus was praying alone, the disciples came to him. "Who do the crowds say I am?" he asked them.

[19] "Some say that you are John the Baptist," they answered. "Others say that you are Elijah, while others say that one of the prophets of long ago has come back to life."

[20] "What about you?" he asked them. "Who do you say I am?"

Peter answered, "You are God's Messiah."

Jesus Speaks about his Suffering and Death

[21] Then Jesus gave them strict orders not to tell this to anyone. [22] He also said to them, "The Son of Man must suffer much and be rejected by the elders, the chief priests, and the teachers of the Law. He will be put to death, but three days later he will be raised to life."

[23] And he said to them all, "Anyone who wants to come with me must forget self, take up their cross every day, and follow me. [24] For whoever wants to save their own life will lose it, but whoever loses their life for my sake will save it. [25] Will people gain anything if they win the whole world but are themselves lost or defeated? Of course not! [26] If people are ashamed of me and of my teaching, then the Son of Man will be ashamed of them when he comes in his glory and in the glory of the Father and of the holy angels. [27] I assure you that there are some here who will not die until they have seen the Kingdom of God."

The Transfiguration

[28] About a week after he had said these things, Jesus took Peter, John, and James with him and went up a hill to pray. [29] While he was praying, his face changed its appearance, and his clothes became dazzling white. [30] Suddenly two men were there talking with him. They were Moses and Elijah, [31] who appeared in heavenly glory and talked with Jesus about the way in which he would soon fulfil God's purpose by dying in Jerusalem. [32] Peter and his companions were sound asleep, but they woke up and saw Jesus' glory and the two men who were standing with him. [33] As the men were leaving Jesus, Peter said to him, "Master, how good it is that we are here! We will make three tents,

one for you, one for Moses, and one for Elijah." (He did not really know what he was saying.)

[34] While he was still speaking, a cloud appeared and covered them with its shadow; and the disciples were afraid as the cloud came over them. [35] A voice said from the cloud, "This is my Son, whom I have chosen — listen to him!"

[36] When the voice stopped, there was Jesus all alone. The disciples kept quiet about all this, and told no one at that time anything they had seen.

Jesus Heals a Boy with an Evil Spirit

[37] The next day Jesus and the three disciples went down from the hill, and a large crowd met Jesus. [38] A man shouted from the crowd, "Teacher! I beg you, look at my son — my only son! [39] A spirit attacks him with a sudden shout and throws him into a fit, so that he foams at the mouth; it keeps on hurting him and will hardly let him go! [40] I begged your disciples to drive it out, but they couldn't."

[41] Jesus answered, "How unbelieving and wrong you people are! How long must I stay with you? How long do I have to put up with you?" Then he said to the man, "Bring your son here."

[42] As the boy was coming, the demon knocked him to the ground and threw him into a fit. Jesus gave a command to the evil spirit, healed the boy, and gave him back to his father. [43] All the people were amazed at the mighty power of God.

Jesus Speaks Again about his Death

The people were still marvelling at everything Jesus was doing, when he said to his disciples, [44] "Don't forget what I am about to tell you! The Son of Man is going to be handed over to the power of human beings." [45] But the disciples did not know what this meant. It had been hidden from them so that they could not understand it, and they were afraid to ask him about the matter.

Who is the Greatest?

[46] An argument broke out among the disciples as to which one of them was the greatest. [47] Jesus knew what they were thinking, so he took a child, stood him by his side, [48] and said to them, "Whoever welcomes this child in my name, welcomes me; and whoever welcomes me, also welcomes the one who sent me. For the one who is least among you all is the greatest."

Whoever is not Against You is For You

[49] John spoke up, "Master, we saw a man driving out demons in your name, and we told him to stop, because he doesn't belong to our group."

[50] "Do not try to stop him," Jesus said to him and to the other disciples, "because whoever is not against you is for you."

A Samaritan Village Refuses to Receive Jesus

[51] As the time drew near when Jesus would be taken up to heaven, he made up his mind and set out on his way to Jerusalem. [52] He sent messengers ahead of him, who went into a village in Samaria to get everything ready for him. [53] But the people there would not receive him, because it was clear that he was on his way to Jerusalem. [54] When the disciples James and John saw this, they said, "Lord, do you want us to call fire down from heaven to destroy them?"

[55] Jesus turned and rebuked them. [56] Then Jesus and his disciples went on to another village.

The Would-be Followers of Jesus

[57] As they went on their way, a man said to Jesus, "I will follow you wherever you go."

[58] Jesus said to him, "Foxes have holes, and birds have nests, but the Son of Man has nowhere to lie down and rest."

[59] He said to another man, "Follow me."

But that man said, "Sir, first let me go back and bury my father."

[60] Jesus answered, "Let the dead bury their own dead. You go and proclaim the Kingdom of God."

[61] Someone else said, "I will follow you, sir; but first let me go and say goodbye to my family."

[62] Jesus said to him, "Anyone who starts to plough and then keeps looking back is of no use to the Kingdom of God."

Jesus Sends Out the 72

[1] After this the Lord chose another 72 men and sent them out two by two, to go ahead of him to every town and place where he himself was about to go. [2] He said to them, "There is a large harvest, but few workers to gather it in. Pray to the owner of the harvest that he will send out workers to gather in his harvest. [3] Go! I am sending you like lambs among wolves. [4] Don't take a purse or a beggar's bag or shoes; don't stop to greet anyone on the road. [5] Whenever you go into a house, first say, 'Peace be with this house.' [6] If a peace-loving person lives there, let your greeting of peace remain on him; if not, take back your greeting of peace. [7] Stay in that same house, eating and drinking whatever they offer you, for workers should be given their pay. Don't move round from one house to another. [8] Whenever you go into a town and are made welcome, eat what is set before you, [9] heal the sick in that town, and say to the people there, 'The Kingdom of God has come near you.' [10] But whenever you go into a town and are not welcomed, go out in the streets and say, [11] 'Even the dust from your town that sticks to our feet we wipe off against you. But remember that the Kingdom of God has come near you!' [12] I assure you that on Judgement Day God will show more mercy to Sodom than to that town!

The Unbelieving Towns

[13] "How terrible it will be for you, Chorazin! How terrible for you too, Bethsaida! If the miracles which were performed in you had been performed in Tyre and Sidon, the people there would long ago have sat down, put on sackcloth, and sprinkled ashes on themselves, to show that they had turned from their sins! [14] God will show more mercy on Judgement Day to Tyre and Sidon than to you. [15] And as for you, Capernaum! Did you want to lift yourself up to heaven? You will be thrown down to hell!"

[16] Jesus said to his disciples, "Whoever listens to you listens to me; whoever rejects you rejects me; and whoever rejects me rejects the one who sent me."

The Return of the 72

[17] The 72 men came back in great joy. "Lord," they said, "even the demons obeyed us when we gave them a command in your name!"

[18] Jesus answered them, "I saw Satan fall like lightning from heaven. [19] Listen! I have given you authority, so that you can walk on snakes

and scorpions and overcome all the power of the Enemy, and nothing will hurt you. [20] But don't be glad because the evil spirits obey you; rather be glad because your names are written in heaven."

Jesus Rejoices

[21] At that time Jesus was filled with joy by the Holy Spirit and said, "Father, Lord of heaven and earth! I thank you because you have shown to the unlearned what you have hidden from the wise and learned. Yes, Father, this was how you wanted it to happen.

[22] "My Father has given me all things. No one knows who the Son is except the Father, and no one knows who the Father is except the Son and those to whom the Son chooses to reveal him."

[23] Then Jesus turned to the disciples and said to them privately, "How fortunate you are to see the things you see! [24] I tell you that many prophets and kings wanted to see what you see, but they could not, and to hear what you hear, but they did not."

The Parable of the Good Samaritan

[25] A teacher of the Law came up and tried to trap Jesus. "Teacher," he asked, "what must I do to receive eternal life?"

[26] Jesus answered him, "What do the Scriptures say? How do you interpret them?"

[27] The man answered, " 'Love the Lord your God with all your heart, with all your soul, with all your strength, and with all your mind'; and 'Love your neighbour as you love yourself.' "

[28] "You are right," Jesus replied; "do this and you will live."

[29] But the teacher of the Law wanted to justify himself, so he asked Jesus, "Who is my neighbour?"

[30] Jesus answered, "There was once a man who was going down from Jerusalem to Jericho when robbers attacked him, stripped him, and beat him up, leaving him half dead. [31] It so happened that a priest was going down that road; but when he saw the man, he walked on by, on the other side. [32] In the same way a Levite also came along, went over and looked at the man, and then walked on by, on the other side. [33] But a Samaritan who was travelling that way came upon the man, and when he saw him, his heart was filled with pity. [34] He went over to him, poured oil and wine on his wounds and bandaged them; then he put the man on his own animal and took him to an inn, where he took

care of him. [35] The next day he took out two silver coins and gave them to the innkeeper. 'Take care of him,' he told the innkeeper, 'and when I come back this way, I will pay you whatever else you spend on him.' "

[36] And Jesus concluded, "In your opinion, which one of these three acted like a neighbour towards the man attacked by the robbers?"

[37] The teacher of the Law answered, "The one who was kind to him."

Jesus replied, "You go, then, and do the same."

Jesus Visits Martha and Mary

[38] As Jesus and his disciples went on their way, he came to a village where a woman named Martha welcomed him in her home. [39] She had a sister named Mary, who sat down at the feet of the Lord and listened to his teaching. [40] Martha was upset over all the work she had to do, so she came and said, "Lord, don't you care that my sister has left me to do all the work by myself? Tell her to come and help me!"

[41] The Lord answered her, "Martha, Martha! You are worried and troubled over so many things, [42] but just one is needed. Mary has chosen the right thing, and it will not be taken away from her."

Jesus' Teaching on Prayer

[1] One day Jesus was praying in a certain place. When he had finished, one of his disciples said to him, "Lord, teach us to pray, just as John taught his disciples."

[2] Jesus said to them, "When you pray, say this:

> 'Father:
>> May your holy name be honoured;
>> may your Kingdom come.
>
> [3] Give us day by day the food we need.
>
> [4] Forgive us our sins,
>> for we forgive everyone who does us wrong.
>> And do not bring us to hard testing.'"

[5] And Jesus said to his disciples, "Suppose one of you should go to a friend's house at midnight and say, 'Friend, let me borrow three loaves of bread. [6] A friend of mine who is on a journey has just come to my house, and I haven't got any food for him!' [7] And suppose your friend should answer from inside, 'Don't bother me! The door is already locked, and my children and I are in bed. I can't get up and give you anything.' [8] Well, what then? I tell you that even if he will not get up and give you the bread because you are his friend, yet he will get up and give you everything you need because you are not ashamed to keep on asking.

[9] "And so I say to you: ask, and you will receive; seek, and you will find; knock, and the door will be opened to you. [10] For all those who ask will receive, and those who seek will find, and the door will be opened to anyone who knocks. [11] Would any of you who are fathers give your son a snake when he asks for fish? [12] Or would you give him a scorpion when he asks for an egg? [13] Bad as you are, you know how to give good things to your children. How much more, then, will the Father in heaven give the Holy Spirit to those who ask him!"

Jesus and Beelzebul

[14] Jesus was driving out a demon that could not talk; and when the demon went out, the man began to talk. The crowds were amazed, [15] but some of the people said, "It is Beelzebul, the chief of the demons, who gives him the power to drive them out."

[16] Others wanted to trap Jesus, so they asked him to perform a miracle to show that God approved of him. [17] But Jesus knew what they were thinking, so he said to them, "Any country that divides itself into

groups which fight each other will not last very long; a family divided against itself falls apart. [18] So if Satan's kingdom has groups fighting each other, how can it last? You say that I drive out demons because Beelzebul gives me the power to do so. [19] If this is how I drive them out, how do your followers drive them out? Your own followers prove that you are wrong! [20] No, it is rather by means of God's power that I drive out demons, and this proves that the Kingdom of God has already come to you.

[21] "When a strong man, with all his weapons ready, guards his own house, all his belongings are safe. [22] But when a stronger man attacks him and defeats him, he carries away all the weapons the owner was depending on and divides up what he stole.

[23] "Anyone who is not for me is really against me; anyone who does not help me gather is really scattering.

The Return of the Evil Spirit

[24] "When an evil spirit goes out of a person, it travels over dry country looking for a place to rest. If it can't find one, it says to itself, 'I will go back to my house.' [25] So it goes back and finds the house clean and tidy. [26] Then it goes out and brings seven other spirits even worse than itself, and they come and live there. So when it is all over, that person is in a worse state than he was at the beginning."

True Happiness

[27] When Jesus had said this, a woman spoke up from the crowd and said to him, "How happy is the woman who bore you and nursed you!"

[28] But Jesus answered, "Rather, how happy are those who hear the word of God and obey it!"

The Demand for a Miracle

[29] As the people crowded round Jesus, he went on to say, "How evil are the people of this day! They ask for a miracle, but none will be given them except the miracle of Jonah. [30] In the same way that the prophet Jonah was a sign for the people of Nineveh, so the Son of Man will be a sign for the people of this day. [31] On Judgement Day the Queen of Sheba will stand up and accuse the people of today, because she travelled all the way from her country to listen to King Solomon's wise teaching; and I tell you there is something here greater than Solomon. [32] On Judgement Day the people of Nineveh will stand up and accuse

you, because they turned from their sins when they heard Jonah preach; and I assure you that there is something here greater than Jonah!

The Light of the Body

[33] "No one lights a lamp and then hides it or puts it under a bowl; instead, he puts it on the lampstand, so that people may see the light as they come in. [34] Your eyes are like a lamp for the body. When your eyes are sound, your whole body is full of light; but when your eyes are no good, your whole body will be in darkness. [35] Make certain, then, that the light in you is not darkness. [36] If your whole body is full of light, with no part of it in darkness, it will be bright all over, as when a lamp shines on you with its brightness."

Jesus Accuses the Pharisees and the Teachers of the Law

[37] When Jesus finished speaking, a Pharisee invited him to eat with him; so he went in and sat down to eat. [38] The Pharisee was surprised when he noticed that Jesus had not washed before eating. [39] So the Lord said to him, "Now then, you Pharisees clean the outside of your cup and plate, but inside you are full of violence and evil. [40] Fools! Did not God, who made the outside, also make the inside? [41] But give what is in your cups and plates to the poor, and everything will be ritually clean for you.

[42] "How terrible for you Pharisees! You give God a tenth of the seasoning herbs, such as mint and rue and all the other herbs, but you neglect justice and love for God. These you should practise, without neglecting the others.

[43] "How terrible for you Pharisees! You love the reserved seats in the synagogues and to be greeted with respect in the market places. [44] How terrible for you! You are like unmarked graves which people walk on without knowing it."

[45] One of the teachers of the Law said to him, "Teacher, when you say this, you insult us too!"

[46] Jesus answered, "How terrible also for you teachers of the Law! You put loads on people's backs which are hard to carry, but you yourselves will not stretch out a finger to help them carry those loads. [47] How terrible for you! You make fine tombs for the prophets — the very prophets your ancestors murdered. [48] You yourselves admit, then, that you approve of what your ancestors did; they murdered the prophets,

and you build their tombs. ⁴⁹For this reason the Wisdom of God said, 'I will send them prophets and messengers; they will kill some of them and persecute others.' ⁵⁰So the people of this time will be punished for the murder of all the prophets killed since the creation of the world, ⁵¹from the murder of Abel to the murder of Zechariah, who was killed between the altar and the Holy Place. Yes, I tell you, the people of this time will be punished for them all!

⁵²"How terrible for you teachers of the Law! You have kept the key that opens the door to the house of knowledge; you yourselves will not go in, and you stop those who are trying to go in!"

⁵³When Jesus left that place, the teachers of the Law and the Pharisees began to criticize him bitterly and ask him questions about many things, ⁵⁴trying to lay traps for him and catch him saying something wrong.

A Warning against Hypocrisy

¹As thousands of people crowded together, so that they were stepping on each other, Jesus said first to his disciples, "Be on guard against the yeast of the Pharisees — I mean their hypocrisy. ²Whatever is covered up will be uncovered, and every secret will be made known. ³So then, whatever you have said in the dark will be heard in broad daylight, and whatever you have whispered in private in a closed room will be shouted from the housetops.

Whom to Fear

⁴"I tell you, my friends, do not be afraid of those who kill the body but cannot afterwards do anything worse. ⁵I will show you whom to fear: fear God, who, after killing, has the authority to throw into hell. Believe me, he is the one you must fear!

⁶"Aren't five sparrows sold for two pennies? Yet not one sparrow is forgotten by God. ⁷Even the hairs of your head have all been counted. So do not be afraid; you are worth much more than many sparrows!

Confessing and Rejecting Christ

⁸"I assure you that for those who declare publicly that they belong to me, the Son of Man will do the same before the angels of God. ⁹But those who reject me publicly, the Son of Man will also reject before the angels of God.

¹⁰"Whoever says a word against the Son of Man can be forgiven; but those who say evil things against the Holy Spirit will not be forgiven.

¹¹"When they bring you to be tried in the synagogues or before governors or rulers, do not be worried about how you will defend yourself or what you will say. ¹²For the Holy Spirit will teach you at that time what you should say."

The Parable of the Rich Fool

¹³A man in the crowd said to Jesus, "Teacher, tell my brother to divide with me the property our father left us."

¹⁴Jesus answered him, "My friend, who gave me the right to judge or to divide the property between you two?" ¹⁵And he went on to say to them all, "Watch out and guard yourselves from every kind of greed; because a person's true life is not made up of the things he owns, no matter how rich he may be."

[16] Then Jesus told them this parable: "There was once a rich man who had land which bore good crops. [17] He began to think to himself, 'I haven't anywhere to keep all my crops. What can I do? [18] This is what I will do,' he told himself; 'I will tear down my barns and build bigger ones, where I will store my corn and all my other goods. [19] Then I will say to myself, Lucky man! You have all the good things you need for many years. Take life easy, eat, drink, and enjoy yourself!' [20] But God said to him, 'You fool! This very night you will have to give up your life; then who will get all these things you have kept for yourself?'"

[21] And Jesus concluded, "This is how it is with those who pile up riches for themselves but are not rich in God's sight."

Trust in God

[22] Then Jesus said to the disciples, "And so I tell you not to worry about the food you need to stay alive or about the clothes you need for your body. [23] Life is much more important than food, and the body much more important than clothes. [24] Look at the crows: they don't sow seeds or gather a harvest; they don't have storerooms or barns; God feeds them! You are worth so much more than birds! [25] Can any of you live a bit longer by worrying about it? [26] If you can't manage even such a small thing, why worry about the other things? [27] Look how the wild flowers grow: they don't work or make clothes for themselves. But I tell you that not even King Solomon with all his wealth had clothes as beautiful as one of these flowers. [28] It is God who clothes the wild grass — grass that is here today and gone tomorrow, burnt up in the oven. Won't he be all the more sure to clothe you? How little faith you have!

[29] "So don't be all upset, always concerned about what you will eat and drink. [30] (For the pagans of this world are always concerned about all these things.) Your Father knows that you need these things. [31] Instead, be concerned with his Kingdom, and he will provide you with these things.

Riches in Heaven

[32] "Do not be afraid, little flock, for your Father is pleased to give you the Kingdom. [33] Sell all your belongings and give the money to the poor. Provide for yourselves purses that don't wear out, and save your riches in heaven, where they will never decrease, because no thief can get to them, and no moth can destroy them. [34] For your heart will always be where your riches are.

Watchful Servants

35 "Be ready for whatever comes, dressed for action and with your lamps lit, 36 like servants who are waiting for their master to come back from a wedding feast. When he comes and knocks, they will open the door for him at once. 37 How happy are those servants whose master finds them awake and ready when he returns! I tell you, he will take off his coat, ask them to sit down, and will wait on them. 38 How happy they are if he finds them ready, even if he should come at midnight or even later! 39 And you can be sure that if the owner of a house knew the time when the thief would come, he would not let the thief break into his house. 40 And you, too, must be ready, because the Son of Man will come at an hour when you are not expecting him."

The Faithful or the Unfaithful Servant

41 Peter said, "Lord, does this parable apply to us, or do you mean it for everyone?"

42 The Lord answered, "Who, then, is the faithful and wise servant? He is the one that his master will put in charge, to run the household and give the other servants their share of the food at the proper time. 43 How happy that servant is if his master finds him doing this when he comes home! 44 Indeed, I tell you, the master will put that servant in charge of all his property. 45 But if that servant says to himself that his master is taking a long time to come back and if he begins to beat the other servants, both the men and the women, and eats and drinks and gets drunk, 46 then the master will come back one day when the servant does not expect him and at a time he does not know. The master will cut him in pieces and make him share the fate of the disobedient.

47 "The servant who knows what his master wants him to do, but does not get himself ready and do it, will be punished with a heavy whipping. 48 But the servant who does not know what his master wants, and yet does something for which he deserves a whipping, will be punished with a light whipping. Much is required from the person to whom much is given; much more is required from the person to whom much more is given.

Jesus the Cause of Division

49 "I came to set the earth on fire, and how I wish it were already kindled! 50 I have a baptism to receive, and how distressed I am until it is over! 51 Do you suppose that I came to bring peace to the world? No,

not peace, but division. [52] From now on a family of five will be divided, three against two and two against three. [53] Fathers will be against their sons, and sons against their fathers; mothers will be against their daughters, and daughters against their mothers; mothers-in-law will be against their daughters-in-law, and daughters-in-law against their mothers-in-law."

Understanding the Time

[54] Jesus said also to the people, "When you see a cloud coming up in the west, at once you say that it is going to rain — and it does. [55] And when you feel the south wind blowing, you say that it is going to get hot — and it does. [56] Hypocrites! You can look at the earth and the sky and predict the weather; why, then, don't you know the meaning of this present time?

Settle with your Opponent

[57] "Why do you not judge for yourselves the right thing to do? [58] If someone brings a lawsuit against you and takes you to court, do your best to settle the dispute with them before you get to court. If you don't, they will drag you before the judge, who will hand you over to the police, and you will be put in jail. [59] There you will stay, I tell you, until you pay the last penny of your fine."

Turn from your Sins or Die

[1] At that time some people were there who told Jesus about the Galileans whom Pilate had killed while they were offering sacrifices to God. [2] Jesus answered them, "Because those Galileans were killed in that way, do you think it proves that they were worse sinners than all the other Galileans? [3] No indeed! And I tell you that if you do not turn from your sins, you will all die as they did. [4] What about those eighteen people in Siloam who were killed when the tower fell on them? Do you suppose this proves that they were worse than all the other people living in Jerusalem? [5] No indeed! And I tell you that if you do not turn from your sins, you will all die as they did."

The Parable of the Unfruitful Fig Tree

[6] Then Jesus told them this parable: "There was once a man who had a fig tree growing in his vineyard. He went looking for figs on it but found none. [7] So he said to his gardener, 'Look, for three years I have been coming here looking for figs on this fig tree, and I haven't found any. Cut it down! Why should it go on using up the soil?' [8] But the gardener answered, 'Leave it alone, sir, just one more year; I will dig round it and put in some manure. [9] Then if the tree bears figs next year, so much the better; if not, then you can have it cut down.'"

Jesus Heals a Crippled Woman on the Sabbath

[10] One Sabbath Jesus was teaching in a synagogue. [11] A woman there had an evil spirit that had made her ill for eighteen years; she was bent over and could not straighten up at all. [12] When Jesus saw her, he called out to her, "Woman, you are free from your illness!" [13] He placed his hands on her, and at once she straightened herself up and praised God.

[14] The official of the synagogue was angry that Jesus had healed on the Sabbath, so he spoke up and said to the people, "There are six days in which we should work; so come during those days and be healed, but not on the Sabbath!"

[15] The Lord answered him, "You hypocrites! Any one of you would untie your ox or your donkey from the stall and take it out to give it water on the Sabbath. [16] Now here is this descendant of Abraham whom Satan has kept bound up for eighteen years; should she not be released on the Sabbath?" [17] His answer made his enemies ashamed of themselves, while the people rejoiced over all the wonderful things that he did.

The Parable of the Mustard Seed

[18] Jesus asked, "What is the Kingdom of God like? What shall I compare it with? [19] It is like this. A man takes a mustard seed and sows it in his field. The plant grows and becomes a tree, and the birds make their nests in its branches."

The Parable of the Yeast

[20] Again Jesus asked, "What shall I compare the Kingdom of God with? [21] It is like this. A woman takes some yeast and mixes it with forty litres of flour until the whole batch of dough rises."

The Narrow Door

[22] Jesus went through towns and villages, teaching the people and making his way towards Jerusalem. [23] Someone asked him, "Sir, will just a few people be saved?"

Jesus answered them, [24] "Do your best to go in through the narrow door; because many people will surely try to go in but will not be able. [25] The master of the house will get up and close the door; then when you stand outside and begin to knock on the door and say, 'Open the door for us, sir!' he will answer you, 'I don't know where you come from!' [26] Then you will answer, 'We ate and drank with you; you taught in our town!' [27] But he will say again, 'I don't know where you come from. Get away from me, all you wicked people!' [28] How you will cry and grind your teeth when you see Abraham, Isaac, and Jacob, and all the prophets in the Kingdom of God, while you are thrown out! [29] People will come from the east and the west, from the north and the south, and sit down at the feast in the Kingdom of God. [30] Then those who are now last will be first, and those who are now first will be last."

Jesus' Love for Jerusalem

[31] At that same time some Pharisees came to Jesus and said to him, "You must get out of here and go somewhere else, because Herod wants to kill you."

[32] Jesus answered them, "Go and tell that fox: 'I am driving out demons and performing cures today and tomorrow, and on the third day I shall finish my work.' [33] Yet I must be on my way today, tomorrow, and the next day; it is not right for a prophet to be killed anywhere except in Jerusalem.

³⁴ "Jerusalem, Jerusalem! You kill the prophets, you stone the messengers God has sent you! How many times have I wanted to put my arms round all your people, just as a hen gathers her chicks under her wings, but you would not let me! ³⁵ And so your Temple will be abandoned. I assure you that you will not see me until the time comes when you say, 'God bless him who comes in the name of the Lord.'"

Jesus Heals a Sick Man

[1] One Sabbath Jesus went to eat a meal at the home of one of the leading Pharisees; and people were watching Jesus closely. [2] A man whose legs and arms were swollen came to Jesus, [3] and Jesus asked the teachers of the Law and the Pharisees, "Does our Law allow healing on the Sabbath or not?"

[4] But they would not say anything. Jesus took the man, healed him, and sent him away. [5] Then he said to them, "If any one of you had a son or an ox that happened to fall in a well on a Sabbath, would you not pull them out at once on the Sabbath itself?"

[6] But they were not able to answer him about this.

Humility and Hospitality

[7] Jesus noticed how some of the guests were choosing the best places, so he told this parable to all of them: [8] "When someone invites you to a wedding feast, do not sit down in the best place. It could happen that someone more important than you has been invited, [9] and your host, who invited both of you, would have to come and say to you, 'Let him have this place.' Then you would be embarrassed and have to sit in the lowest place. [10] Instead, when you are invited, go and sit in the lowest place, so that your host will come to you and say, 'Come on up, my friend, to a better place.' This will bring you honour in the presence of all the other guests. [11] For all those who make themselves great will be humbled, and those who humble themselves will be made great."

[12] Then Jesus said to his host, "When you give a lunch or a dinner, do not invite your friends or your brothers or your relatives or your rich neighbours — for they will invite you back, and in this way you will be paid for what you did. [13] When you give a feast, invite the poor, the crippled, the lame, and the blind; [14] and you will be blessed, because they are not able to pay you back. God will repay you on the day the good people rise from death."

The Parable of the Great Feast

[15] When one of the men sitting at table heard this, he said to Jesus, "How happy are those who will sit down at the feast in the Kingdom of God!"

[16] Jesus said to him, "There was once a man who was giving a great feast to which he invited many people. [17] When it was time for the feast, he sent his servant to tell his guests, 'Come, everything is ready!'

18 But they all began, one after another, to make excuses. The first one told the servant, 'I have bought a field and must go and look at it; please accept my apologies.' 19 Another one said, 'I have bought five pairs of oxen and am on my way to try them out; please accept my apologies.' 20 Another one said, 'I have just got married, and for that reason I cannot come.'

21 "The servant went back and told all this to his master. The master was furious and said to his servant, 'Hurry out to the streets and alleys of the town, and bring back the poor, the crippled, the blind, and the lame.' 22 Soon the servant said, 'Your order has been carried out, sir, but there is room for more.' 23 So the master said to the servant, 'Go out to the country roads and lanes and make people come in, so that my house will be full. 24 I tell you all that none of those who were invited will taste my dinner!' "

The Cost of Being a Disciple

25 Once when large crowds of people were going along with Jesus, he turned and said to them, 26 "Those who come to me cannot be my disciples unless they love me more than they love father and mother, wife and children, brothers and sisters, and themselves as well. 27 Those who do not carry their own cross and come after me cannot be my disciples.

28 "If one of you is planning to build a tower, you sit down first and work out what it will cost, to see if you have enough money to finish the job. 29 If you don't, you will not be able to finish the tower after laying the foundation; and all who see what happened will laugh at you. 30 'This man began to build but can't finish the job!' they will say.

31 "If a king goes out with 10,000 men to fight another king who comes against him with 20,000 men, he will sit down first and decide if he is strong enough to face that other king. 32 If he isn't, he will send messengers to meet the other king, to ask for terms of peace while he is still a long way off. 33 In the same way," concluded Jesus, "none of you can be my disciple unless you give up everything you have.

Worthless Salt

34 "Salt is good, but if it loses its saltiness, there is no way to make it salty again. 35 It is no good for the soil or for the manure heap; it is thrown away. Listen, then, if you have ears!"

"The servant went back and told all this to his master. The master was furious and said to his servant, 'Hurry out to the streets and alleys of the town, and bring back the poor, the crippled, the blind, and the lame.'"

Luke 14.21

Reflect

The whole of the Bible can be read as an invitation from God to come and live a life full of joy and purpose. In this story, called a parable, God is the master of the house, the house is the kingdom of God, and we are both the servant and the people being invited. Jesus is using this parable to show that the invitation of God is for everybody.

Earlier in this story people are giving their excuses to reject the invitation – and we can often do that too. Sometimes we don't make enough time to respond to God's invitation. But God desperately wants us to come – 'make people come in' as the Bible says. This shows a God who isn't just inviting us, but a God who loves us so much that he really wants us all to come, and we're drawn by this love, not forced unwillingly. It's not an open house – we're asked to come by name. And for this loving God a half-empty house is a failure – there can be no empty seats at the table.

This is an invitation where the poor, the sick, the outcasts, are welcomed as equals, as kings at the master's table. So how do you answer this kind of invitation, for you and for others around you? Are you happy to change your plans to come along to God's great party – or are you going to make an excuse not to go?

Pray

Lord Jesus,
you do not reject anyone;
you invite me by name to sit with you.
You want no one to be alone,
but for us all to be with you.
Open my heart to this invitation,
an invitation to live life well.
Amen

Act

This invitation is for all – to not be alone, to not be rejected.
But we're often too busy to accept an invitation, or to offer one
to someone else. Think about your week ahead: can you make
space to just spend time with someone you don't normally,
either by accepting their invitation or offering your own?

The Lost Sheep

[1] One day when many tax collectors and other outcasts came to listen to Jesus, [2] the Pharisees and the teachers of the Law started grumbling, "This man welcomes outcasts and even eats with them!" [3] So Jesus told them this parable:

[4] "Suppose one of you has a hundred sheep and loses one of them — what do you do? You leave the other 99 sheep in the pasture and go looking for the one that got lost until you find it. [5] When you find it, you are so happy that you put it on your shoulders [6] and carry it back home. Then you call your friends and neighbours together and say to them, 'I am so happy I found my lost sheep. Let us celebrate!' [7] In the same way, I tell you, there will be more joy in heaven over one sinner who repents than over 99 respectable people who do not need to repent.

The Lost Coin

[8] "Or suppose a woman who has ten silver coins loses one of them — what does she do? She lights a lamp, sweeps her house, and looks carefully everywhere until she finds it. [9] When she finds it, she calls her friends and neighbours together, and says to them, 'I am so happy I found the coin I lost. Let us celebrate!' [10] In the same way, I tell you, the angels of God rejoice over one sinner who repents."

The Lost Son

[11] Jesus went on to say, "There was once a man who had two sons. [12] The younger one said to him, 'Father, give me my share of the property now.' So the man divided his property between his two sons. [13] After a few days the younger son sold his part of the property and left home with the money. He went to a country far away, where he wasted his money in reckless living. [14] He spent everything he had. Then a severe famine spread over that country, and he was left without a thing. [15] So he went to work for one of the citizens of that country, who sent him out to his farm to take care of the pigs. [16] He wished he could fill himself with the bean pods the pigs ate, but no one gave him anything to eat. [17] At last he came to his senses and said, 'All my father's hired workers have more than they can eat, and here I am about to starve! [18] I will get up and go to my father and say, Father, I have sinned against God and against you. [19] I am no longer fit to be called your son; treat me as one of your hired workers.' [20] So he got up and started back to his father.

"He was still a long way from home when his father saw him; his heart was filled with pity, and he ran, threw his arms round his son, and kissed him. 21 'Father,' the son said, 'I have sinned against God and against you. I am no longer fit to be called your son.' 22 But the father called his servants. 'Hurry!' he said. 'Bring the best robe and put it on him. Put a ring on his finger and shoes on his feet. 23 Then go and get the prize calf and kill it, and let us celebrate with a feast! 24 For this son of mine was dead, but now he is alive; he was lost, but now he has been found.' And so the feasting began.

25 "In the meantime the elder son was out in the field. On his way back, when he came close to the house, he heard the music and dancing. 26 So he called one of the servants and asked him, 'What's going on?' 27 'Your brother has come back home,' the servant answered, 'and your father has killed the prize calf, because he got him back safe and sound.'

28 "The elder brother was so angry that he would not go into the house; so his father came out and begged him to come in. 29 But he answered his father, 'Look, all these years I have worked for you like a slave, and I have never disobeyed your orders. What have you given me? Not even a goat for me to have a feast with my friends! 30 But this son of yours wasted all your property on prostitutes, and when he comes back home, you kill the prize calf for him!' 31 'My son,' the father answered, 'you are always here with me, and everything I have is yours. 32 But we had to celebrate and be happy, because your brother was dead, but now he is alive; he was lost, but now he has been found.'"

The Shrewd Manager

[1] Jesus said to his disciples, "There was once a rich man who had a servant who managed his property. The rich man was told that the manager was wasting his master's money, [2] so he called him in and said, 'What is this I hear about you? Hand in a complete account of your handling of my property, because you cannot be my manager any longer.' [3] The servant said to himself, 'My master is going to dismiss me from my job. What shall I do? I am not strong enough to dig ditches, and I am ashamed to beg. [4] Now I know what I will do! Then when my job is gone, I shall have friends who will welcome me in their homes.'

[5] "So he called in all the people who were in debt to his master. He asked the first one, 'How much do you owe my master?' [6] '100 barrels of olive oil,' he answered. 'Here is your account,' the manager told him; 'sit down and write fifty.' [7] Then he asked another one, 'And you — how much do you owe?' 'A thousand sacks of wheat,' he answered. 'Here is your account,' the manager told him; 'write 800.'

[8] "As a result the master of this dishonest manager praised him for doing such a shrewd thing; because the people of this world are much more shrewd in handling their affairs than the people who belong to the light."

[9] And Jesus went on to say, "And so I tell you: make friends for yourselves with worldly wealth, so that when it gives out, you will be welcomed in the eternal home. [10] Whoever is faithful in small matters will be faithful in large ones; whoever is dishonest in small matters will be dishonest in large ones. [11] If, then, you have not been faithful in handling worldly wealth, how can you be trusted with true wealth? [12] And if you have not been faithful with what belongs to someone else, who will give you what belongs to you?

[13] "No servant can be the slave of two masters; such a servant will hate one and love the other or will be loyal to one and despise the other. You cannot serve both God and money."

Some Sayings of Jesus

[14] When the Pharisees heard all this, they sneered at Jesus, because they loved money. [15] Jesus said to them, "You are the ones who make yourselves look right in other people's sight, but God knows your hearts. For the things that are considered of great value by human beings are worth nothing in God's sight.

[16] "The Law of Moses and the writings of the prophets were in effect up to the time of John the Baptist; since then the Good News about the Kingdom of God is being told, and everyone forces their way in. [17] But it is easier for heaven and earth to disappear than for the smallest detail of the Law to be done away with.

[18] "Any man who divorces his wife and marries another woman commits adultery; and the man who marries a divorced woman commits adultery.

The Rich Man and Lazarus

[19] "There was once a rich man who dressed in the most expensive clothes and lived in great luxury every day. [20] There was also a poor man named Lazarus, covered with sores, who used to be brought to the rich man's door, [21] hoping to eat the bits of food that fell from the rich man's table. Even the dogs would come and lick his sores.

[22] "The poor man died and was carried by the angels to sit beside Abraham at the feast in heaven. The rich man died and was buried, [23] and in Hades, where he was in great pain, he looked up and saw Abraham, far away, with Lazarus at his side. [24] So he called out, 'Father Abraham! Take pity on me, and send Lazarus to dip his finger in some water and cool my tongue, because I am in great pain in this fire!'

[25] "But Abraham said, 'Remember, my son, that in your lifetime you were given all the good things, while Lazarus got all the bad things. But now he is enjoying himself here, while you are in pain. [26] Besides all that, there is a deep pit lying between us, so that those who want to cross over from here to you cannot do so, nor can anyone cross over to us from where you are.' [27] The rich man said, 'Then I beg you, father Abraham, send Lazarus to my father's house, [28] where I have five brothers. Let him go and warn them so that they, at least, will not come to this place of pain.'

[29] "Abraham said, 'Your brothers have Moses and the prophets to warn them; your brothers should listen to what they say.' [30] The rich man answered, 'That is not enough, father Abraham! But if someone were to rise from death and go to them, then they would turn from their sins.' [31] But Abraham said, 'If they will not listen to Moses and the prophets, they will not be convinced even if someone were to rise from death.'"

Sin

[1] Jesus said to his disciples, "Things that make people fall into sin are bound to happen, but how terrible for the one who makes them happen! [2] It would be better for him if a large millstone were tied round his neck and he were thrown into the sea than for him to cause one of these little ones to sin. [3] So watch what you do!

"If your brother sins, rebuke him, and if he repents, forgive him. [4] If he sins against you seven times in one day, and each time he comes to you saying, 'I repent,' you must forgive him."

Faith

[5] The apostles said to the Lord, "Make our faith greater."

[6] The Lord answered, "If you had faith as big as a mustard seed, you could say to this mulberry tree, 'Pull yourself up by the roots and plant yourself in the sea!' and it would obey you.

A Servant's Duty

[7] "Suppose one of you has a servant who is ploughing or looking after the sheep. When he comes in from the field, do you tell him to hurry and eat his meal? [8] Of course not! Instead, you say to him, 'Get my supper ready, then put on your apron and wait on me while I eat and drink; after that you may have your meal.' [9] The servant does not deserve thanks for obeying orders, does he? [10] It is the same with you; when you have done all you have been told to do, say, 'We are ordinary servants; we have only done our duty.'"

Jesus Heals Ten Men

[11] As Jesus made his way to Jerusalem, he went along the border between Samaria and Galilee. [12] He was going into a village when he was met by ten men suffering from a dreaded skin disease. They stood at a distance [13] and shouted, "Jesus! Master! Take pity on us!"

[14] Jesus saw them and said to them, "Go and let the priests examine you."

On the way they were made clean. [15] When one of them saw that he was healed, he came back, praising God in a loud voice. [16] He threw himself to the ground at Jesus' feet and thanked him. The man was a Samaritan. [17] Jesus said, "There were ten men who were healed; where are the other nine? [18] Why is this foreigner the only one who came back to give thanks to God?" [19] And Jesus said to him, "Get up and go; your faith has made you well."

The Coming of the Kingdom

[20] Some Pharisees asked Jesus when the Kingdom of God would come. His answer was, "The Kingdom of God does not come in such a way as to be seen. [21] No one will say, 'Look, here it is!' or, 'There it is!'; because the Kingdom of God is within you."

[22] Then he said to the disciples, "The time will come when you will wish you could see one of the days of the Son of Man, but you will not see it. [23] There will be those who will say to you, 'Look, over there!' or, 'Look, over here!' But don't go out looking for it. [24] As the lightning flashes across the sky and lights it up from one side to the other, so will the Son of Man be in his day. [25] But first he must suffer much and be rejected by the people of this day. [26] As it was in the time of Noah so shall it be in the days of the Son of Man. [27] Everybody kept on eating and drinking, and men and women married, up to the very day Noah went into the boat and the flood came and killed them all. [28] It will be as it was in the time of Lot. Everybody kept on eating and drinking, buying and selling, planting and building. [29] On the day Lot left Sodom, fire and sulphur rained down from heaven and killed them all. [30] That is how it will be on the day the Son of Man is revealed.

[31] "On that day someone who is on the roof of his house must not go down into the house to get any belongings; in the same way anyone who is out in the field must not go back to the house. [32] Remember Lot's wife! [33] Whoever tries to save his own life will lose it; whoever loses his life will save it. [34] On that night, I tell you, there will be two people sleeping in the same bed: one will be taken away, the other will be left behind. [35] Two women will be grinding corn together: one will be taken away, the other will be left behind."

[37] The disciples asked him, "Where, Lord?"

Jesus answered, "Wherever there is a dead body, the vultures will gather."

The Parable of the Widow and the Judge

[1] Then Jesus told his disciples a parable to teach them that they should always pray and never become discouraged. [2] "In a certain town there was a judge who neither feared God nor respected people. [3] And there was a widow in that same town who kept coming to him and pleading for her rights, saying, 'Help me against my opponent!' [4] For a long time the judge refused to act, but at last he said to himself, 'Even though I don't fear God or respect people, [5] yet because of all the trouble this widow is giving me, I will see to it that she gets her rights. If I don't, she will keep on coming and finally wear me out!' "

[6] And the Lord continued, "Listen to what that corrupt judge said. [7] Now, will God not judge in favour of his own people who cry to him day and night for help? Will he be slow to help them? [8] I tell you, he will judge in their favour and do it quickly. But will the Son of Man find faith on earth when he comes?"

The Parable of the Pharisee and the Tax Collector

[9] Jesus also told this parable to people who were sure of their own goodness and despised everybody else. [10] "Once there were two men who went up to the Temple to pray: one was a Pharisee, the other a tax collector.

[11] "The Pharisee stood apart by himself and prayed, 'I thank you, God, that I am not greedy, dishonest, or an adulterer, like everybody else. I thank you that I am not like that tax collector over there. [12] I fast two days a week, and I give you a tenth of all my income.'

[13] "But the tax collector stood at a distance and would not even raise his face to heaven, but beat on his breast and said, 'God, have pity on me, a sinner!' [14] I tell you," said Jesus, "the tax collector, and not the Pharisee, was in the right with God when he went home. For all who make themselves great will be humbled, and all who humble themselves will be made great."

Jesus Blesses Little Children

[15] Some people brought their babies to Jesus for him to place his hands on them. The disciples saw them and scolded them for doing so, [16] but Jesus called the children to him and said, "Let the children come to me and do not stop them, because the Kingdom of God belongs to such as these. [17] Remember this! Whoever does not receive the Kingdom of God like a child will never enter it."

The Rich Man

[18] A Jewish leader asked Jesus, "Good Teacher, what must I do to receive eternal life?"

[19] "Why do you call me good?" Jesus asked him. "No one is good except God alone. [20] You know the commandments: 'Do not commit adultery; do not commit murder; do not steal; do not accuse anyone falsely; respect your father and your mother.'"

[21] The man replied, "Ever since I was young, I have obeyed all these commandments."

[22] When Jesus heard this, he said to him, "There is still one more thing you need to do. Sell all you have and give the money to the poor, and you will have riches in heaven; then come and follow me." [23] But when the man heard this, he became very sad, because he was very rich.

[24] Jesus saw that he was sad and said, "How hard it is for rich people to enter the Kingdom of God! [25] It is much harder for a rich person to enter the Kingdom of God than for a camel to go through the eye of a needle."

[26] The people who heard him asked, "Who, then, can be saved?"

[27] Jesus answered, "What is humanly impossible is possible for God."

[28] Then Peter said, "Look! We have left our homes to follow you."

[29] "Yes," Jesus said to them, "and I assure you that anyone who leaves home or wife or brothers or parents or children for the sake of the Kingdom of God [30] will receive much more in this present age and eternal life in the age to come."

Jesus Speaks a Third Time about his Death

[31] Jesus took the twelve disciples aside and said to them, "Listen! We are going to Jerusalem where everything the prophets wrote about the Son of Man will come true. [32] He will be handed over to the Gentiles, who will mock him, insult him, and spit on him. [33] They will whip him and kill him, but three days later he will rise to life."

[34] But the disciples did not understand any of these things; the meaning of the words was hidden from them, and they did not know what Jesus was talking about.

Jesus Heals a Blind Beggar

[35] As Jesus was coming near Jericho, there was a blind man sitting by the road, begging. [36] When he heard the crowd passing by, he asked, "What is this?"

37 "Jesus of Nazareth is passing by," they told him.

38 He cried out, "Jesus! Son of David! Take pity on me!"

39 The people in front scolded him and told him to be quiet. But he shouted even more loudly, "Son of David! Take pity on me!"

40 So Jesus stopped and ordered the blind man to be brought to him. When he came near, Jesus asked him, 41 "What do you want me to do for you?"

"Sir," he answered, "I want to see again."

42 Jesus said to him, "Then see! Your faith has made you well."

43 At once he was able to see, and he followed Jesus, giving thanks to God. When the crowd saw it, they all praised God.

When Jesus heard this, he said to him, "There is still one more thing you need to do. Sell all you have and give the money to the poor, and you will have riches in heaven; then come and follow me."

Luke 18.22

Reflect

Jesus was never afraid to challenge those he met. The stories he told and the things he did often challenged those around him with a completely new and different idea of how the world should be. In this meeting Jesus sees that this man, who has learned and obeyed all of God's laws since childhood, still has room to grow in kindness and selflessness. He is challenging him that the journey of a true disciple is lifelong, and that he cannot have two masters, God and money.

It might not be money for you – but we all have a blind spot, that one thing which, for all our talk and hope, we let turn us away from the path we know we should be following. It could be a bad behaviour, an addiction, a vice.

This is a challenge for all of us – to recognise that we can't have two masters. It's not easy, but it's an invitation and an opportunity to change, to grow, to be a better version of ourselves, to show the love we need to show, the love that Jesus shows to us.

If we are truly to follow Jesus, we must be committed to his challenge to show love and kindness, to give time to those who need it, to be always ready to do good.

Pray

Lord Jesus, the radical who changes the world,
strengthen me to face the challenges that lie before me.
Shine a light on my blind spots,
and help me overcome the things that keep me from your path.
Amen

Act

Is there something in your life right now that is stopping you
from answering that challenge of love? It could be an activity,
a behaviour, or it could be a barrier inside you, something
that holds you back. It might feel like a wall that you can't
get through. Can you change that behaviour, go without that
activity, or break down that barrier, even just for a day? Can you
imagine what it would be like without it – to be free of it? Focus
on how that makes you feel.

Jesus and Zacchaeus

[1] Jesus went on into Jericho and was passing through. [2] There was a chief tax collector there named Zacchaeus, who was rich. [3] He was trying to see who Jesus was, but he was a little man and could not see Jesus because of the crowd. [4] So he ran ahead of the crowd and climbed a sycomore tree to see Jesus, who was going to pass that way. [5] When Jesus came to that place, he looked up and said to Zacchaeus, "Hurry down, Zacchaeus, because I must stay in your house today."

[6] Zacchaeus hurried down and welcomed him with great joy. [7] All the people who saw it started grumbling, "This man has gone as a guest to the home of a sinner!"

[8] Zacchaeus stood up and said to the Lord, "Listen, sir! I will give half my belongings to the poor, and if I have cheated anyone, I will pay back four times as much."

[9] Jesus said to him, "Salvation has come to this house today, for this man, also, is a descendant of Abraham. [10] The Son of Man came to seek and to save the lost."

The Parable of the Gold Coins

[11] While the people were listening to this, Jesus continued and told them a parable. He was now almost at Jerusalem, and they supposed that the Kingdom of God was just about to appear. [12] So he said, "There was once a man of high rank who was going to a country far away to be made king, after which he planned to come back home. [13] Before he left, he called his ten servants and gave them each a gold coin and told them, 'See what you can earn with this while I am gone.' [14] Now, his own people hated him, and so they sent messengers after him to say, 'We don't want this man to be our king.'

[15] "The man was made king and came back. At once he ordered his servants to appear before him, in order to find out how much they had earned. [16] The first one came and said, 'Sir, I have earned ten gold coins with the one you gave me.' [17] 'Well done,' he said; 'you are a good servant! Since you were faithful in small matters, I will put you in charge of ten cities.' [18] The second servant came and said, 'Sir, I have earned five gold coins with the one you gave me.' [19] To this one he said, 'You will be in charge of five cities.'

[20] "Another servant came and said, 'Sir, here is your gold coin; I kept it hidden in a handkerchief. [21] I was afraid of you, because you are a hard man. You take what is not yours and reap what you did not sow.' [22] He

said to him, 'You bad servant! I will use your own words to condemn you! You know that I am a hard man, taking what is not mine and reaping what I have not sown. [23] Well, then, why didn't you put my money in the bank? Then I would have received it back with interest when I returned.'

[24] "Then he said to those who were standing there, 'Take the gold coin away from him and give it to the servant who has ten coins.' [25] But they said to him, 'Sir, he already has ten coins!' [26] 'I tell you,' he replied, 'that to all those who have something, even more will be given; but those who have nothing, even the little that they have will be taken away from them. [27] Now, as for those enemies of mine who did not want me to be their king, bring them here and kill them in my presence!'"

The Triumphant Approach to Jerusalem

[28] After Jesus said this, he went on ahead of them to Jerusalem. [29] As he came near Bethphage and Bethany at the Mount of Olives, he sent two disciples ahead [30] with these instructions: "Go to the village there ahead of you; as you go in, you will find a colt tied up that has never been ridden. Untie it and bring it here. [31] If someone asks you why you are untying it, tell him that the Master needs it."

[32] They went on their way and found everything just as Jesus had told them. [33] As they were untying the colt, its owners said to them, "Why are you untying it?"

[34] "The Master needs it," they answered, [35] and they took the colt to Jesus. Then they threw their cloaks over the animal and helped Jesus get on. [36] As he rode on, people spread their cloaks on the road.

[37] When he came near Jerusalem, at the place where the road went down the Mount of Olives, the large crowd of his disciples began to thank God and praise him in loud voices for all the great things that they had seen: [38] "God bless the king who comes in the name of the Lord! Peace in heaven and glory to God!"

[39] Then some of the Pharisees in the crowd spoke to Jesus. "Teacher," they said, "command your disciples to be quiet!"

[40] Jesus answered, "I tell you that if they keep quiet, the stones themselves will start shouting."

Jesus Weeps over Jerusalem

[41] He came closer to the city, and when he saw it, he wept over it, [42] saying, "If you only knew today what is needed for peace! But

now you cannot see it! [43] The time will come when your enemies will surround you with barricades, blockade you, and close in on you from every side. [44] They will completely destroy you and the people within your walls; not a single stone will they leave in its place, because you did not recognize the time when God came to save you!"

Jesus Goes to the Temple

[45] Then Jesus went into the Temple and began to drive out the merchants, [46] saying to them, "It is written in the Scriptures that God said, 'My Temple will be a house of prayer.' But you have turned it into a hideout for thieves!"

[47] Every day Jesus taught in the Temple. The chief priests, the teachers of the Law, and the leaders of the people wanted to kill him, [48] but they could not find a way to do it, because all the people kept listening to him, not wanting to miss a single word.

The Question about Jesus' Authority

¹ One day when Jesus was in the Temple teaching the people and preaching the Good News, the chief priests and the teachers of the Law, together with the elders, came ² and said to him, "Tell us, what right have you to do these things? Who gave you this right?"

³ Jesus answered them, "Now let me ask you a question. Tell me, ⁴ did John's right to baptize come from God or from human beings?"

⁵ They started to argue among themselves, "What shall we say? If we say, 'From God,' he will say, 'Why, then, did you not believe John?' ⁶ But if we say 'From human beings,' this whole crowd here will stone us, because they are convinced that John was a prophet." ⁷ So they answered, "We don't know where it came from."

⁸ And Jesus said to them, "Neither will I tell you, then, by what right I do these things."

The Parable of the Tenants in the Vineyard

⁹ Then Jesus told the people this parable: "There was once a man who planted a vineyard, let it out to tenants, and then left home for a long time. ¹⁰ When the time came to gather the grapes, he sent a slave to the tenants to receive from them his share of the harvest. But the tenants beat the slave and sent him back without a thing. ¹¹ So he sent another slave; but the tenants beat him also, treated him shamefully, and sent him back without a thing. ¹² Then he sent a third slave; the tenants wounded him, too, and threw him out. ¹³ Then the owner of the vineyard said, 'What shall I do? I will send my own dear son; surely they will respect him!' ¹⁴ But when the tenants saw him, they said to one another, 'This is the owner's son. Let's kill him, and his property will be ours!' ¹⁵ So they threw him out of the vineyard and killed him.

"What, then, will the owner of the vineyard do to the tenants?" Jesus asked. ¹⁶ "He will come and kill those men, and hand the vineyard over to other tenants."

When the people heard this, they said, "Surely not!"

¹⁷ Jesus looked at them and asked, "What, then, does this scripture mean?

'The stone which the builders rejected as worthless
    turned out to be the most important of all.'

¹⁸ Everyone who falls on that stone will be cut to pieces; and if that stone falls on someone, it will crush him to dust."

The Question about Paying Taxes

[19] The teachers of the Law and the chief priests tried to arrest Jesus on the spot, because they knew that he had told this parable against them; but they were afraid of the people. [20] So they looked for an opportunity. They bribed some men to pretend they were sincere, and they sent them to trap Jesus with questions, so that they could hand him over to the authority and power of the Roman Governor. [21] These spies said to Jesus, "Teacher, we know that what you say and teach is right. We know that you pay no attention to anyone's status, but teach the truth about God's will for people. [22] Tell us, is it against our Law for us to pay taxes to the Roman Emperor, or not?"

[23] But Jesus saw through their trick and said to them, [24] "Show me a silver coin. Whose face and name are these on it?"

"The Emperor's," they answered.

[25] So Jesus said, "Well, then, pay the Emperor what belongs to the Emperor, and pay God what belongs to God."

[26] There before the people they could not catch him out in anything, so they kept quiet, amazed at his answer.

The Question about Rising from Death

[27] Then some Sadducees, who say that people will not rise from death, came to Jesus and said, [28] "Teacher, Moses wrote this law for us: 'If a man dies and leaves a wife but no children, that man's brother must marry the widow so that they can have children who will be considered the dead man's children.' [29] Once there were seven brothers; the eldest got married and died without having children. [30] Then the second one married the woman, [31] and then the third. The same thing happened to all seven — they died without having children. [32] Last of all, the woman died. [33] Now, on the day when the dead rise to life, whose wife will she be? All seven of them had married her."

[34] Jesus answered them, "The men and women of this age marry, [35] but the men and women who are worthy to rise from death and live in the age to come will not then marry. [36] They will be like angels and cannot die. They are the children of God, because they have risen from death. [37] And Moses clearly proves that the dead are raised to life. In the passage about the burning bush he speaks of the Lord as 'the God of Abraham, the God of Isaac, and the God of Jacob.' [38] He is the God of the living, not of the dead, for to him all are alive."

³⁹ Some of the teachers of the Law spoke up, "A good answer, Teacher!" ⁴⁰ For they did not dare ask him any more questions.

The Question about the Messiah

⁴¹ Jesus asked them, "How can it be said that the Messiah will be the descendant of David? ⁴² For David himself says in the book of Psalms,

> 'The Lord said to my Lord:
>> Sit here on my right
> ⁴³   until I put your enemies as a footstool under your feet.'

⁴⁴ David called him 'Lord'; how, then, can the Messiah be David's descendant?"

Jesus Warns against the Teachers of the Law

⁴⁵ As all the people listened to him, Jesus said to his disciples, ⁴⁶ "Be on your guard against the teachers of the Law, who like to walk about in their long robes and love to be greeted with respect in the market place; who choose the reserved seats in the synagogues and the best places at feasts; ⁴⁷ who take advantage of widows and rob them of their homes, and then make a show of saying long prayers! Their punishment will be all the worse!"

The Widow's Offering

[1] Jesus looked round and saw rich people dropping their gifts in the temple treasury, [2] and he also saw a very poor widow dropping in two little copper coins. [3] He said, "I tell you that this poor widow put in more than all the others. [4] For the others offered their gifts from what they had to spare of their riches; but she, poor as she is, gave all she had to live on."

Jesus Speaks of the Destruction of the Temple

[5] Some of the disciples were talking about the Temple, how beautiful it looked with its fine stones and the gifts offered to God. Jesus said, [6] "All this you see — the time will come when not a single stone here will be left in its place; every one will be thrown down."

Troubles and Persecutions

[7] "Teacher," they asked, "when will this be? And what will happen in order to show that the time has come for it to take place?"

[8] Jesus said, "Be on guard; don't be deceived. Many men, claiming to speak for me, will come and say, 'I am he!' and, 'The time has come!' But don't follow them. [9] Don't be afraid when you hear of wars and revolutions; such things must happen first, but they do not mean that the end is near."

[10] He went on to say, "Countries will fight each other; kingdoms will attack one another. [11] There will be terrible earthquakes, famines, and plagues everywhere; there will be strange and terrifying things coming from the sky. [12] Before all these things take place, however, you will be arrested and persecuted; you will be handed over to be tried in synagogues and be put in prison; you will be brought before kings and rulers for my sake. [13] This will be your chance to tell the Good News. [14] Make up your minds beforehand not to worry about how you will defend yourselves, [15] because I will give you such words and wisdom that none of your enemies will be able to refute or contradict what you say. [16] You will be handed over by your parents, your brothers, your relatives, and your friends; and some of you will be put to death. [17] Everyone will hate you because of me. [18] But not a single hair from your heads will be lost. [19] Stand firm, and you will save yourselves.

Jesus Speaks of the Destruction of Jerusalem

[20] "When you see Jerusalem surrounded by armies, then you will know that it will soon be destroyed. [21] Then those who are in Judea must

run away to the hills; those who are in the city must leave, and those who are out in the country must not go into the city. [22] For those will be 'The Days of Punishment', to make all that the Scriptures say come true. [23] How terrible it will be in those days for women who are pregnant and for mothers with little babies! Terrible distress will come upon this land, and God's punishment will fall on this people. [24] Some will be killed by the sword, and others will be taken as prisoners to all countries; and the heathen will trample over Jerusalem until their time is up.

The Coming of the Son of Man

[25] "There will be strange things happening to the sun, the moon, and the stars. On earth whole countries will be in despair, afraid of the roar of the sea and the raging tides. [26] People will faint from fear as they wait for what is coming over the whole earth, for the powers in space will be driven from their courses. [27] Then the Son of Man will appear, coming in a cloud with great power and glory. [28] When these things begin to happen, stand up and raise your heads, because your salvation is near."

The Lesson of the Fig Tree

[29] Then Jesus told them this parable: "Think of the fig tree and all the other trees. [30] When you see their leaves beginning to appear, you know that summer is near. [31] In the same way, when you see these things happening, you will know that the Kingdom of God is about to come.

[32] "Remember that all these things will take place before the people now living have all died. [33] Heaven and earth will pass away, but my words will never pass away.

The Need to Watch

[34] "Be on your guard! Don't let yourselves become occupied with too much feasting and drinking and with the worries of this life, or that Day may suddenly catch you [35] like a trap. For it will come upon all people everywhere on earth. [36] Be on the alert and pray always that you will have the strength to go safely through all those things that will happen and to stand before the Son of Man."

[37] Jesus spent those days teaching in the Temple, and when evening came, he would go out and spend the night on the Mount of Olives. [38] Early each morning all the people went to the Temple to listen to him.

The Plot against Jesus

[1] The time was near for the Festival of Unleavened Bread, which is called the Passover. [2] The chief priests and the teachers of the Law were afraid of the people, and so they were trying to find a way of putting Jesus to death secretly.

Judas Agrees to Betray Jesus

[3] Then Satan entered Judas, called Iscariot, who was one of the twelve disciples. [4] So Judas went off and spoke with the chief priests and the officers of the temple guard about how he could betray Jesus to them. [5] They were pleased and offered to pay him money. [6] Judas agreed to it and started looking for a good chance to hand Jesus over to them without the people knowing about it.

Jesus Prepares to Eat the Passover Meal

[7] The day came during the Festival of Unleavened Bread when the lambs for the Passover meal were to be killed. [8] Jesus sent off Peter and John with these instructions: "Go and get the Passover meal ready for us to eat."

[9] "Where do you want us to get it ready?" they asked him.

[10] He answered, "As you go into the city, a man carrying a jar of water will meet you. Follow him into the house that he enters, [11] and say to the owner of the house: 'The Teacher says to you, Where is the room where my disciples and I will eat the Passover meal?' [12] He will show you a large furnished room upstairs, where you will get everything ready."

[13] They went off and found everything just as Jesus had told them, and they prepared the Passover meal.

The Lord's Supper

[14] When the hour came, Jesus took his place at the table with the apostles. [15] He said to them, "I have wanted so much to eat this Passover meal with you before I suffer! [16] For I tell you, I will never eat it until it is given its full meaning in the Kingdom of God."

[17] Then Jesus took a cup, gave thanks to God, and said, "Take this and share it among yourselves. [18] I tell you that from now on I will not drink this wine until the Kingdom of God comes."

[19] Then he took a piece of bread, gave thanks to God, broke it, and gave it to them, saying, "This is my body, which is given for you. Do this

in memory of me." [20] In the same way, he gave them the cup after the supper, saying, "This cup is God's new covenant sealed with my blood, which is poured out for you.

[21] "But, look! The one who betrays me is here at the table with me! [22] The Son of Man will die as God has decided, but how terrible for that man who betrays him!"

[23] Then they began to ask among themselves which one of them it could be who was going to do this.

The Argument about Greatness

[24] An argument broke out among the disciples as to which one of them should be thought of as the greatest. [25] Jesus said to them, "The kings of the pagans have power over their people, and the rulers claim the title 'Friends of the People'. [26] But this is not the way it is with you; rather, the greatest one among you must be like the youngest, and the leader must be like the servant. [27] Who is greater, the one who sits down to eat or the one who serves? The one who sits down, of course. But I am among you as one who serves.

[28] "You have stayed with me all through my trials; [29] and just as my Father has given me the right to rule, so I will give you the same right. [30] You will eat and drink at my table in my Kingdom, and you will sit on thrones to rule over the twelve tribes of Israel.

Jesus Predicts Peter's Denial

[31] "Simon, Simon! Listen! Satan has received permission to test all of you, to separate the good from the bad, as a farmer separates the wheat from the chaff. [32] But I have prayed for you, Simon, that your faith will not fail. And when you turn back to me, you must strengthen your brothers."

[33] Peter answered, "Lord, I am ready to go to prison with you and to die with you!"

[34] "I tell you, Peter," Jesus said, "the cock will not crow tonight until you have said three times that you do not know me."

Purse, Bag, and Sword

[35] Then Jesus asked his disciples, "When I sent you out that time without purse, bag, or shoes, did you lack anything?"

"Not a thing," they answered.

36 "But now," Jesus said, "whoever has a purse or a bag must take it; and whoever has no sword must sell his coat and buy one. 37 For I tell you that the scripture which says, 'He shared the fate of criminals,' must come true about me, because what was written about me is coming true."

38 The disciples said, "Look! Here are two swords, Lord!"

"That is enough!" he replied.

Jesus Prays on the Mount of Olives

39 Jesus left the city and went, as he usually did, to the Mount of Olives; and the disciples went with him. 40 When he arrived at the place, he said to them, "Pray that you will not fall into temptation."

41 Then he went off from them about the distance of a stone's throw and knelt down and prayed. 42 "Father," he said, "if you will, take this cup of suffering away from me. Not my will, however, but your will be done." 43 An angel from heaven appeared to him and strengthened him. 44 In great anguish he prayed even more fervently; his sweat was like drops of blood falling to the ground.

45 Rising from his prayer, he went back to the disciples and found them asleep, worn out by their grief. 46 He said to them, "Why are you sleeping? Get up and pray that you will not fall into temptation."

The Arrest of Jesus

47 Jesus was still speaking when a crowd arrived, led by Judas, one of the twelve disciples. He came up to Jesus to kiss him. 48 But Jesus said, "Judas, is it with a kiss that you betray the Son of Man?"

49 When the disciples who were with Jesus saw what was going to happen, they asked, "Shall we use our swords, Lord?" 50 And one of them struck the High Priest's slave and cut off his right ear.

51 But Jesus said, "Enough of this!" He touched the man's ear and healed him.

52 Then Jesus said to the chief priests and the officers of the temple guard and the elders who had come there to get him, "Did you have to come with swords and clubs, as though I were an outlaw? 53 I was with you in the Temple every day, and you did not try to arrest me. But this is your hour to act, when the power of darkness rules."

Peter Denies Jesus

[54] They arrested Jesus and took him away into the house of the High Priest; and Peter followed at a distance. [55] A fire had been lit in the centre of the courtyard, and Peter joined those who were sitting round it. [56] When one of the servant women saw him sitting there at the fire, she looked straight at him and said, "This man too was with Jesus!"

[57] But Peter denied it, "Woman, I don't even know him!"

[58] After a little while a man noticed Peter and said, "You are one of them, too!"

But Peter answered, "Man, I am not!"

[59] And about an hour later another man insisted strongly, "There isn't any doubt that this man was with Jesus, because he also is a Galilean!"

[60] But Peter answered, "Man, I don't know what you are talking about!"

At once, while he was still speaking, a cock crowed. [61] The Lord turned round and looked straight at Peter, and Peter remembered that the Lord had said to him, "Before the cock crows tonight, you will say three times that you do not know me." [62] Peter went out and wept bitterly.

Jesus is Mocked and Beaten

[63] The men who were guarding Jesus mocked him and beat him. [64] They blindfolded him and asked him, "Who hit you? Guess!" [65] And they said many other insulting things to him.

Jesus is Brought before the Council

[66] When day came, the elders, the chief priests, and the teachers of the Law met together, and Jesus was brought before the Council. [67] "Tell us," they said, "are you the Messiah?"

He answered, "If I tell you, you will not believe me; [68] and if I ask you a question, you will not answer. [69] But from now on the Son of Man will be seated on the right of Almighty God."

[70] They all said, "Are you, then, the Son of God?"

He answered them, "You say that I am."

[71] And they said, "We don't need any witnesses! We ourselves have heard what he said!"

Jesus is Brought before Pilate

[1] The whole group rose up and took Jesus before Pilate, [2] where they began to accuse him: "We caught this man misleading our people, telling them not to pay taxes to the Emperor and claiming that he himself is the Messiah, a king."

[3] Pilate asked him, "Are you the king of the Jews?"

"So you say," answered Jesus.

[4] Then Pilate said to the chief priests and the crowds, "I find no reason to condemn this man."

[5] But they insisted even more strongly, "With his teaching he is starting a riot among the people all through Judea. He began in Galilee and now has come here."

Jesus is Sent to Herod

[6] When Pilate heard this, he asked, "Is this man a Galilean?" [7] When he learnt that Jesus was from the region ruled by Herod, he sent him to Herod, who was also in Jerusalem at that time. [8] Herod was very pleased when he saw Jesus, because he had heard about him and had been wanting to see him for a long time. He was hoping to see Jesus perform some miracle. [9] So Herod asked Jesus many questions, but Jesus made no answer. [10] The chief priests and the teachers of the Law stepped forward and made strong accusations against Jesus. [11] Herod and his soldiers mocked Jesus and treated him with contempt; then they put a fine robe on him and sent him back to Pilate. [12] On that very day Herod and Pilate became friends; before this they had been enemies.

Jesus is Sentenced to Death

[13] Pilate called together the chief priests, the leaders, and the people, [14] and said to them, "You brought this man to me and said that he was misleading the people. Now, I have examined him here in your presence, and I have not found him guilty of any of the crimes you accuse him of. [15] Nor did Herod find him guilty, for he sent him back to us. There is nothing this man has done to deserve death. [16] So I will have him whipped and let him go."

[18] The whole crowd cried out, "Kill him! Set Barabbas free for us!" [19] (Barabbas had been put in prison for a riot that had taken place in the city, and for murder.)

[20] Pilate wanted to set Jesus free, so he appealed to the crowd again.
[21] But they shouted back, "Crucify him! Crucify him!"

[22] Pilate said to them the third time, "But what crime has he committed? I cannot find anything he has done to deserve death! I will have him whipped and set him free."

[23] But they kept on shouting at the top of their voices that Jesus should be crucified, and finally their shouting succeeded. [24] So Pilate passed the sentence on Jesus that they were asking for. [25] He set free the man they wanted, the one who had been put in prison for riot and murder, and he handed Jesus over for them to do as they wished.

Jesus is Crucified

[26] The soldiers led Jesus away, and as they were going, they met a man from Cyrene named Simon who was coming into the city from the country. They seized him, put the cross on him, and made him carry it behind Jesus.

[27] A large crowd of people followed him; among them were some women who were weeping and wailing for him. [28] Jesus turned to them and said, "Women of Jerusalem! Don't cry for me, but for yourselves and your children. [29] For the days are coming when people will say, 'How lucky are the women who never had children, who never bore babies, who never nursed them!' [30] That will be the time when people will say to the mountains, 'Fall on us!' and to the hills, 'Hide us!' [31] For if such things as these are done when the wood is green, what will happen when it is dry?"

[32] Two other men, both of them criminals, were also led out to be put to death with Jesus. [33] When they came to the place called "The Skull", they crucified Jesus there, and the two criminals, one on his right and the other on his left. [34] Jesus said, "Forgive them, Father! They don't know what they are doing."

They divided his clothes among themselves by throwing dice. [35] The people stood there watching while the Jewish leaders jeered at him: "He saved others; let him save himself if he is the Messiah whom God has chosen!"

[36] The soldiers also mocked him: they came up to him and offered him cheap wine, [37] and said, "Save yourself if you are the king of the Jews!"

[38] Above him were written these words: "This is the King of the Jews."

[39] One of the criminals hanging there hurled insults at him: "Aren't you the Messiah? Save yourself and us!"

[40] The other one, however, rebuked him, saying, "Don't you fear God? You received the same sentence he did. [41] Ours, however, is only right, because we are getting what we deserve for what we did; but he has done no wrong." [42] And he said to Jesus, "Remember me, Jesus, when you come as King!"

[43] Jesus said to him, "I promise you that today you will be in Paradise with me."

The Death of Jesus

[44-45] It was about twelve o'clock when the sun stopped shining and darkness covered the whole country until three o'clock; and the curtain hanging in the Temple was torn in two. [46] Jesus cried out in a loud voice, "Father! In your hands I place my spirit!" He said this and died.

[47] The army officer saw what had happened, and he praised God, saying, "Certainly he was a good man!"

[48] When the people who had gathered there to watch the spectacle saw what happened, they all went back home, beating their breasts in sorrow. [49] All those who knew Jesus personally, including the women who had followed him from Galilee, stood at a distance to watch.

The Burial of Jesus

[50-51] There was a man named Joseph from Arimathea, a town in Judea. He was a good and honourable man, who was waiting for the coming of the Kingdom of God. Although he was a member of the Council, he had not agreed with their decision and action. [52] He went into the presence of Pilate and asked for the body of Jesus. [53] Then he took the body down, wrapped it in a linen sheet, and placed it in a tomb which had been dug out of solid rock and which had never been used. [54] It was Friday, and the Sabbath was about to begin.

[55] The women who had followed Jesus from Galilee went with Joseph and saw the tomb and how Jesus' body was placed in it. [56] Then they went back home and prepared the spices and perfumes for the body.

On the Sabbath they rested, as the Law commanded.

Jesus said to him, "I promise you that today you will be in Paradise with me."

Reflect

Throughout Luke's telling of Jesus' life, we see someone who restores others. He heals, forgives, supports and challenges.

At his execution Jesus is being crucified between two criminals. These two criminals embody how we view Jesus. One is bullying, even hostile. His heart is closed. Though he is suffering, he bullies those who are suffering too. The other is open, warm, willing to defend the undefended. He admits his mistakes, but he doesn't expect anything in return. He's never even met Jesus, but through him we see Jesus revealed fully, a Jesus who, at the worst point of his suffering, is continuing to love and restore others. With some of his last words, Jesus promises life to that dying criminal, the one who confesses his own wrongdoing. The other, so close physically to the restoration of life on offer through Jesus, all but rejects it.

We're all close to that restoration – it's our choice whether to be open or closed to it, to mock and bully, or to admit our mistakes. We might feel there are areas of our lives that are beyond that love, but we're wrong – Jesus' love can reach every part of who we are, and through us that love can help restore the whole world around us.

Pray

Lord Jesus, the restorer of lives,
soften my heart.
Help me to see that all of me is open to your restoration,
that there is nowhere your love cannot reach.
Work through me to help bring freedom and restoration
to all of creation.
Amen

Act

Consider how you could be part of Jesus' mission of love and
restoration of the world around you. It could be something
personal for you, like opening up to someone you trust about
an area of your life which you think needs restoration, or
it could be something for someone else, such as starting a
conversation with a stranger, or helping to show someone that
no one is beyond Jesus' love.

The Resurrection

[1] Very early on Sunday morning the women went to the tomb, carrying the spices they had prepared. [2] They found the stone rolled away from the entrance to the tomb, [3] so they went in; but they did not find the body of the Lord Jesus. [4] They stood there puzzled about this, when suddenly two men in bright shining clothes stood by them. [5] Full of fear, the women bowed down to the ground, as the men said to them, "Why are you looking among the dead for one who is alive? [6] He is not here; he has been raised. Remember what he said to you while he was in Galilee: [7] 'The Son of Man must be handed over to sinners, be crucified, and three days later rise to life.'"

[8] Then the women remembered his words, [9] returned from the tomb, and told all these things to the eleven disciples and all the rest. [10] The women were Mary Magdalene, Joanna, and Mary the mother of James; they and the other women with them told these things to the apostles. [11] But the apostles thought that what the women said was nonsense, and they did not believe them. [12] But Peter got up and ran to the tomb; he bent down and saw the linen wrappings but nothing else. Then he went back home amazed at what had happened.

The Walk to Emmaus

[13] On that same day two of Jesus' followers were going to a village named Emmaus, about eleven kilometres from Jerusalem, [14] and they were talking to each other about all the things that had happened. [15] As they talked and discussed, Jesus himself drew near and walked along with them; [16] they saw him, but somehow did not recognize him. [17] Jesus said to them, "What are you talking about to each other, as you walk along?"

They stood still, with sad faces. [18] One of them, named Cleopas, asked him, "Are you the only visitor in Jerusalem who doesn't know the things that have been happening there these last few days?"

[19] "What things?" he asked.

"The things that happened to Jesus of Nazareth," they answered. "This man was a prophet and was considered by God and by all the people to be powerful in everything he said and did. [20] Our chief priests and rulers handed him over to be sentenced to death, and he was crucified. [21] And we had hoped that he would be the one who was going to set Israel free! Besides all that, this is now the third day since it happened. [22] Some of the women of our group surprised us; they went at dawn to the tomb, [23] but could not find his body. They came back saying they had seen a vision of angels who told them that he is alive. [24] Some of our group went to the tomb and found it exactly as the women had said, but they did not see him."

[25] Then Jesus said to them, "How foolish you are, how slow you are to believe everything the prophets said! [26] Was it not necessary for the Messiah to suffer these things and then to enter his glory?" [27] And Jesus explained to them what was said about himself in all the Scriptures, beginning with the books of Moses and the writings of all the prophets.

[28] As they came near the village to which they were going, Jesus acted as if he were going farther; [29] but they held him back, saying, "Stay with us; the day is almost over and it is getting dark." So he went in to stay with them. [30] He sat down to eat with them, took the bread, and said the blessing; then he broke the bread and gave it to them. [31] Then their eyes were opened and they recognized him, but he disappeared from their sight. [32] They said to each other, "Wasn't it like a fire burning in us when he talked to us on the road and explained the Scriptures to us?"

[33] They got up at once and went back to Jerusalem, where they found the eleven disciples gathered together with the others [34] and saying, "The Lord is risen indeed! He has appeared to Simon!"

[35] The two then explained to them what had happened on the road, and how they had recognized the Lord when he broke the bread.

Jesus Appears to his Disciples

[36] While the two were telling them this, suddenly the Lord himself stood among them and said to them, "Peace be with you."

[37] They were terrified, thinking that they were seeing a ghost. [38] But he said to them, "Why are you alarmed? Why are these doubts coming up in your minds? [39] Look at my hands and my feet, and see that it is I myself. Feel me, and you will know, for a ghost doesn't have flesh and bones, as you can see I have."

[40] He said this and showed them his hands and his feet. [41] They still could not believe, they were so full of joy and wonder; so he asked them, "Have you anything here to eat?" [42] They gave him a piece of cooked fish, [43] which he took and ate in their presence.

[44] Then he said to them, "These are the very things I told you about while I was still with you: everything written about me in the Law of Moses, the writings of the prophets, and the Psalms had to come true."

⁴⁵ Then he opened their minds to understand the Scriptures, ⁴⁶ and said to them, "This is what is written: the Messiah must suffer and must rise from death three days later, ⁴⁷ and in his name the message about repentance and the forgiveness of sins must be preached to all nations, beginning in Jerusalem. ⁴⁸ You are witnesses of these things. ⁴⁹ And I myself will send upon you what my Father has promised. But you must wait in the city until the power from above comes down upon you."

Jesus is Taken Up to Heaven

⁵⁰ Then he led them out of the city as far as Bethany, where he raised his hands and blessed them. ⁵¹ As he was blessing them, he departed from them and was taken up into heaven. ⁵² They worshipped him and went back into Jerusalem, filled with great joy, ⁵³ and spent all their time in the Temple giving thanks to God.

[1] Dear Theophilus:

In my first book I wrote about all the things that Jesus did and taught from the time he began his work [2] until the day he was taken up to heaven. Before he was taken up, he gave instructions by the power of the Holy Spirit to the men he had chosen as his apostles. [3] For forty days after his death he appeared to them many times in ways that proved beyond doubt that he was alive. They saw him, and he talked with them about the Kingdom of God. [4] And when they came together, he gave them this order: "Do not leave Jerusalem, but wait for the gift I told you about, the gift my Father promised. [5] John baptized with water, but in a few days you will be baptized with the Holy Spirit."

Jesus is Taken Up to Heaven

[6] When the apostles met together with Jesus, they asked him, "Lord, will you at this time give the Kingdom back to Israel?"

[7] Jesus said to them, "The times and occasions are set by my Father's own authority, and it is not for you to know when they will be. [8] But when the Holy Spirit comes upon you, you will be filled with power, and you will be witnesses for me in Jerusalem, in all Judea and Samaria, and to the ends of the earth." [9] After saying this, he was taken up to heaven as they watched him, and a cloud hid him from their sight.

[10] They still had their eyes fixed on the sky as he went away, when two men dressed in white suddenly stood beside them [11] and said, "Galileans, why are you standing there looking up at the sky? This Jesus, who was taken from you into heaven, will come back in the same way that you saw him go to heaven."

Judas' Successor

[12] Then the apostles went back to Jerusalem from the Mount of Olives, which is about a kilometre away from the city. [13] They entered the city and went up to the room where they were staying: Peter, John, James and Andrew, Philip and Thomas, Bartholomew and Matthew, James son of Alphaeus, Simon the Patriot, and Judas son of James. [14] They gathered frequently to pray as a group, together with the women and with Mary the mother of Jesus and with his brothers.

[15] A few days later there was a meeting of the believers, about 120 in all, and Peter stood up to speak. [16] "My fellow-believers," he said, "the scripture had to come true in which the Holy Spirit, speaking through David, made a prediction about Judas, who was the guide for those

who arrested Jesus. [17] Judas was a member of our group, for he had been chosen to have a part in our work."

[18] (With the money that Judas got for his evil act he bought a field, where he fell to his death; he burst open and all his bowels spilt out. [19] All the people living in Jerusalem heard about it, and so in their own language they call that field Akeldama, which means "Field of Blood".)

[20] "For it is written in the book of Psalms:

> 'May his house become empty;
>   may no one live in it.'

It is also written:

> 'May someone else take his place of service.'

[21-22] "So then, someone must join us as a witness to the resurrection of the Lord Jesus. He must be one of the men who were in our group during the whole time that the Lord Jesus travelled about with us, beginning from the time John preached his message of baptism until the day Jesus was taken up from us to heaven."

[23] So they proposed two men: Joseph, who was called Barsabbas (also known as Justus), and Matthias. [24] Then they prayed, "Lord, you know the thoughts of everyone, so show us which of these two you have chosen [25] to serve as an apostle in the place of Judas, who left to go to the place where he belongs." [26] Then they drew lots to choose between the two men, and the one chosen was Matthias, who was added to the group of eleven apostles.

The Coming of the Holy Spirit

[1] When the day of Pentecost came, all the believers were gathered together in one place. [2] Suddenly there was a noise from the sky which sounded like a strong wind blowing, and it filled the whole house where they were sitting. [3] Then they saw what looked like tongues of fire which spread out and touched each person there. [4] They were all filled with the Holy Spirit and began to talk in other languages, as the Spirit enabled them to speak.

[5] There were Jews living in Jerusalem, religious people who had come from every country in the world. [6] When they heard this noise, a large crowd gathered. They were all excited, because each one of them heard the believers speaking in his or her own language. [7] In amazement and wonder they exclaimed, "These people who are talking like this are Galileans! [8] How is it, then, that all of us hear them speaking in our own native languages? [9] We are from Parthia, Media, and Elam; from Mesopotamia, Judea, and Cappadocia; from Pontus and Asia, [10] from Phrygia and Pamphylia, from Egypt and the regions of Libya near Cyrene. Some of us are from Rome, [11] both Jews and Gentiles converted to Judaism, and some of us are from Crete and Arabia — yet all of us hear them speaking in our own languages about the great things that God has done!" [12] Amazed and confused, they kept asking each other, "What does this mean?"

[13] But others made fun of the believers, saying, "These people are drunk!"

Peter's Message

[14] Then Peter stood up with the other eleven apostles and in a loud voice began to speak to the crowd: "Fellow-Jews and all of you who live in Jerusalem, listen to me and let me tell you what this means. [15] These people are not drunk, as you suppose; it is only nine o'clock in the morning. [16] Instead, this is what the prophet Joel spoke about:

[17] 'This is what I will do in the last days, God says:
    I will pour out my Spirit on everyone.
  Your sons and daughters will proclaim my message;
      your young men will see visions,
      and your old men will have dreams.
[18] Yes, even on my servants, both men and women,
      I will pour out my Spirit in those days,
      and they will proclaim my message.

¹⁹ I will perform miracles in the sky above
     and wonders on the earth below.
  There will be blood, fire, and thick smoke;
²⁰   the sun will be darkened,
     and the moon will turn red as blood,
        before the great and glorious Day of the Lord comes.
²¹ And then, whoever calls out to the
        Lord for help will be saved.'

²²"Listen to these words, fellow-Israelites! Jesus of Nazareth was a man whose divine authority was clearly proven to you by all the miracles and wonders which God performed through him. You yourselves know this, for it happened here among you. ²³In accordance with his own plan God had already decided that Jesus would be handed over to you; and you killed him by letting sinful men crucify him. ²⁴But God raised him from death, setting him free from its power, because it was impossible that death should hold him prisoner. ²⁵For David said about him:

  'I saw the Lord before me at all times;
     he is near me, and I will not be troubled.
²⁶ And so I am filled with gladness,
     and my words are full of joy.
  And I, mortal though I am,
     will rest assured in hope,
²⁷ because you will not abandon me in the world of the dead;
     you will not allow your faithful servant to rot in the grave.
²⁸ You have shown me the paths that lead to life,
     and your presence will fill me with joy.'

²⁹"My fellow-Israelites, I must speak to you plainly about our famous ancestor King David. He died and was buried, and his grave is here with us to this very day. ³⁰He was a prophet, and he knew what God had promised him: God had made a vow that he would make one of David's descendants a king, just as David was. ³¹David saw what God was going to do in the future, and so he spoke about the resurrection of the Messiah when he said:

  'He was not abandoned in the world of the dead;
     his body did not rot in the grave.'

³²God has raised this very Jesus from death, and we are all witnesses to this fact. ³³He has been raised to the right-hand side of God, his Father, and has received from him the Holy Spirit, as he had promised.

What you now see and hear is his gift that he has poured out on us. ³⁴ For it was not David who went up into heaven; rather he said:

> 'The Lord said to my Lord:
>> Sit here at my right
> ³⁵ until I put your enemies as a footstool under your feet.'

³⁶ "All the people of Israel, then, are to know for sure that this Jesus, whom you crucified, is the one that God has made Lord and Messiah!"

³⁷ When the people heard this, they were deeply troubled and said to Peter and the other apostles, "What shall we do, brothers?"

³⁸ Peter said to them, "Each one of you must turn away from your sins and be baptized in the name of Jesus Christ, so that your sins will be forgiven; and you will receive God's gift, the Holy Spirit. ³⁹ For God's promise was made to you and your children, and to all who are far away — all whom the Lord our God calls to himself."

⁴⁰ Peter made his appeal to them and with many other words he urged them, saying, "Save yourselves from the punishment coming on this wicked people!" ⁴¹ Many of them believed his message and were baptized, and about 3,000 people were added to the group that day. ⁴² They spent their time in learning from the apostles, taking part in the fellowship, and sharing in the fellowship meals and the prayers.

Life among the Believers

⁴³ Many miracles and wonders were being done through the apostles, and everyone was filled with awe. ⁴⁴ All the believers continued together in close fellowship and shared their belongings with one another. ⁴⁵ They would sell their property and possessions, and distribute the money among all, according to what each one needed. ⁴⁶ Day after day they met as a group in the Temple, and they had their meals together in their homes, eating with glad and humble hearts, ⁴⁷ praising God, and enjoying the good will of all the people. And every day the Lord added to their group those who were being saved.

Peter said to them, "Each one of you must turn away from your sins and be baptized in the name of Jesus Christ, so that your sins will be forgiven; and you will receive God's gift, the Holy Spirit."
Acts 2.38

Reflect

Peter seems like a new man. Not long ago, when questioned after Jesus had been arrested, he'd completely denied that he even knew him. He'd witnessed Jesus being executed and, like many who had followed Jesus, faced the fear and uncertainty that had brought. Then he met the resurrected Jesus and, through the Holy Spirit, that simple fisherman was transformed into a bold preacher to the gathered crowd. He went on an incredible, unexpected journey, and his experience of the Holy Spirit renewed and inspired him – the old Peter, the fisherman, the denier, became the new Peter, the first Christian.

The power of this renewal had been promised by Jesus before he was taken up to heaven, but even then it was hard to know what to expect. Peter wants all his listeners to know that the gift of the Holy Spirit, in whichever unexpected ways it renews and empowers their lives, is freely available to all.

Are you open to the unexpected ways that the Holy Spirit might empower, transform, or guide your life?

Pray

Holy Spirit, the renewer of hearts,
transform the old me into the new me.
Open my eyes to the unexpected ways you act in my life,
and give me strength and determination
to face the challenges ahead.
Amen

Act

Is there a part of your life you think is useless, or something
that makes you feel hopeless? Can you imagine how it might
feel if those things were transformed for the better? Make
space for the Holy Spirit to act unexpectedly in your life, to turn
those things around – useless to useful, hopeless to hopeful.

A Lame Man is Healed

[1] One day Peter and John went to the Temple at three o'clock in the afternoon, the hour for prayer. [2] There at the Beautiful Gate, as it was called, was a man who had been lame all his life. Every day he was carried to the gate to beg for money from the people who were going into the Temple. [3] When he saw Peter and John going in, he begged them to give him something. [4] They looked straight at him, and Peter said, "Look at us!" [5] So he looked at them, expecting to get something from them. [6] But Peter said to him, "I have no money at all, but I give you what I have: in the name of Jesus Christ of Nazareth I order you to get up and walk!" [7] Then he took him by his right hand and helped him up. At once the man's feet and ankles became strong; [8] he jumped up, stood on his feet, and started walking around. Then he went into the Temple with them, walking and jumping and praising God. [9] The people there saw him walking and praising God, [10] and when they recognized him as the beggar who had sat at the Beautiful Gate, they were all surprised and amazed at what had happened to him.

Peter's Message in the Temple

[11] As the man held on to Peter and John in Solomon's Porch, as it was called, the people were amazed and ran to them. [12] When Peter saw the people, he said to them, "Fellow-Israelites, why are you surprised at this, and why do you stare at us? Do you think that it was by means of our own power or godliness that we made this man walk? [13] The God of Abraham, Isaac, and Jacob, the God of our ancestors, has given divine glory to his Servant Jesus. But you handed him over to the authorities, and you rejected him in Pilate's presence, even after Pilate had decided to set him free. [14] He was holy and good, but you rejected him, and instead you asked Pilate to do you the favour of turning loose a murderer. [15] You killed the one who leads to life, but God raised him from death — and we are witnesses to this. [16] It was the power of his name that gave strength to this lame man. What you see and know was done by faith in his name; it was faith in Jesus that has made him well, as you can all see.

[17] "And now, my fellow-Israelites, I know that what you and your leaders did to Jesus was due to your ignorance. [18] God announced long ago through all the prophets that his Messiah had to suffer; and he made it come true in this way. [19] Repent, then, and turn to God, so that he will forgive your sins. If you do, [20] times of spiritual strength will come from the Lord, and he will send Jesus, who is the Messiah

he has already chosen for you. [21] He must remain in heaven until the time comes for all things to be made new, as God announced through his holy prophets who lived long ago. [22] For Moses said, 'The Lord your God will send you a prophet, just as he sent me, and he will be one of your own people. You are to obey everything that he tells you to do. [23] Anyone who does not obey that prophet shall be separated from God's people and destroyed.' [24] And all the prophets who had a message, including Samuel and those who came after him, also announced what has been happening these days. [25] The promises of God through his prophets are for you, and you share in the covenant which God made with your ancestors. As he said to Abraham, 'Through your descendants I will bless all the people on earth.' [26] And so God chose his Servant and sent him first to you, to bless you by making every one of you turn away from your wicked ways."

Peter and John before the Council

[1] Peter and John were still speaking to the people when some priests, the officer in charge of the temple guards, and some Sadducees arrived. [2] They were annoyed because the two apostles were teaching the people that Jesus had risen from death, which proved that the dead will rise to life. [3] So they arrested them and put them in jail until the next day, since it was already late. [4] But many who heard the message believed; and the number of men grew to about 5,000.

[5] The next day the Jewish leaders, the elders, and the teachers of the Law gathered in Jerusalem. [6] They met with the High Priest Annas and with Caiaphas, John, Alexander, and the others who belonged to the High Priest's family. [7] They made the apostles stand before them and asked them, "How did you do this? What power have you got or whose name did you use?"

[8] Peter, full of the Holy Spirit, answered them, "Leaders of the people and elders: [9] if we are being questioned today about the good deed done to the lame man and how he was healed, [10] then you should all know, and all the people of Israel should know, that this man stands here before you completely well through the power of the name of Jesus Christ of Nazareth — whom you crucified and whom God raised from death. [11] Jesus is the one of whom the scripture says:

> 'The stone that you the builders despised
>   turned out to be the most important of all.'

[12] Salvation is to be found through him alone; in all the world there is no one else whom God has given who can save us."

[13] The members of the Council were amazed to see how bold Peter and John were and to learn that they were ordinary men of no education. They realized then that they had been companions of Jesus. [14] But there was nothing that they could say, because they saw the man who had been healed standing there with Peter and John. [15] So they told them to leave the Council room, and then they started discussing among themselves. [16] "What shall we do with these men?" they asked. "Everyone in Jerusalem knows that this extraordinary miracle has been performed by them, and we cannot deny it. [17] But to keep this matter from spreading any further among the people, let us warn these men never again to speak to anyone in the name of Jesus."

[18] So they called them back in and told them that on no condition were they to speak or to teach in the name of Jesus. [19] But Peter and John

answered them, "You yourselves judge which is right in God's sight — to obey you or to obey God. 20 For we cannot stop speaking of what we ourselves have seen and heard." 21 So the Council warned them even more strongly and then set them free. They saw that it was impossible to punish them, because the people were all praising God for what had happened. 22 The man on whom this miracle of healing had been performed was over forty years old.

The Believers Pray for Boldness

23 As soon as Peter and John were set free, they returned to their group and told them what the chief priests and the elders had said. 24 When the believers heard it, they all joined together in prayer to God: "Master and Creator of heaven, earth, and sea, and all that is in them! 25 By means of the Holy Spirit you spoke through our ancestor David, your servant, when he said:

'Why were the Gentiles furious;
    why did people make their useless plots?
26 The kings of the earth prepared themselves,
    and the rulers met together
    against the Lord and his Messiah.'

27 For indeed Herod and Pontius Pilate met together in this city with the Gentiles and the people of Israel against Jesus, your holy Servant, whom you made Messiah. 28 They gathered to do everything that you by your power and will had already decided would happen. 29 And now, Lord, take notice of the threats they have made, and allow us, your servants, to speak your message with all boldness. 30 Stretch out your hand to heal, and grant that wonders and miracles may be performed through the name of your holy Servant Jesus."

31 When they finished praying, the place where they were meeting was shaken. They were all filled with the Holy Spirit and began to proclaim God's message with boldness.

The Believers Share their Possessions

32 The group of believers was one in mind and heart. None of them said that any of their belongings were their own, but they all shared with one another everything they had. 33 With great power the apostles gave witness to the resurrection of the Lord Jesus, and God poured rich blessings on them all. 34 There was no one in the group who was in need. Those who owned fields or houses would sell them, bring

the money received from the sale, ³⁵ and hand it over to the apostles; and the money was distributed to each one according to his need.

³⁶ And so it was that Joseph, a Levite born in Cyprus, whom the apostles called Barnabas (which means "One who Encourages"), ³⁷ sold a field he owned, brought the money, and handed it over to the apostles.

Ananias and Sapphira

[1] But there was a man named Ananias, who with his wife Sapphira sold some property that belonged to them. [2] But with his wife's agreement he kept part of the money for himself and handed the rest over to the apostles. [3] Peter said to him, "Ananias, why did you let Satan take control of you and make you lie to the Holy Spirit by keeping part of the money you received for the property? [4] Before you sold the property, it belonged to you; and after you sold it, the money was yours. Why, then, did you decide to do such a thing? You have not lied to human beings — you have lied to God!" [5] As soon as Ananias heard this, he fell down dead; and all who heard about it were terrified. [6] The young men came in, wrapped up his body, carried him out, and buried him.

[7] About three hours later his wife, not knowing what had happened, came in. [8] Peter asked her, "Tell me, was this the full amount you and your husband received for your property?"

"Yes," she answered, "the full amount."

[9] So Peter said to her, "Why did you and your husband decide to put the Lord's Spirit to the test? The men who buried your husband are now at the door, and they will carry you out too!" [10] At once she fell down at his feet and died. The young men came in and saw that she was dead, so they carried her out and buried her beside her husband. [11] The whole church and all the others who heard of this were terrified.

Miracles and Wonders

[12] Many miracles and wonders were being performed among the people by the apostles. All the believers met together in Solomon's Porch. [13] Nobody outside the group dared to join them, even though the people spoke highly of them. [14] But more and more people were added to the group — a crowd of men and women who believed in the Lord. [15] As a result of what the apostles were doing, sick people were carried out into the streets and placed on beds and mats so that at least Peter's shadow might fall on some of them as he passed by. [16] And crowds of people came in from the towns around Jerusalem, bringing those who were ill or who had evil spirits in them; and they were all healed.

The Apostles are Persecuted

[17] Then the High Priest and all his companions, members of the local party of the Sadducees, became extremely jealous of the apostles;

so they decided to take action. ¹⁸They arrested the apostles and put them in the public jail. ¹⁹But that night an angel of the Lord opened the prison gates, led the apostles out, and said to them, ²⁰"Go and stand in the Temple, and tell the people all about this new life." ²¹The apostles obeyed, and at dawn they entered the Temple and started teaching.

The High Priest and his companions called together all the Jewish elders for a full meeting of the Council; then they sent orders to the prison to have the apostles brought before them. ²²But when the officials arrived, they did not find the apostles in prison, so they returned to the Council and reported, ²³"When we arrived at the jail, we found it locked up tight and all the guards on watch at the gates; but when we opened the gates, we found no one inside!" ²⁴When the chief priests and the officer in charge of the temple guards heard this, they wondered what had happened to the apostles. ²⁵Then a man came in and said to them, "Listen! The men you put in prison are in the Temple teaching the people!" ²⁶So the officer went off with his men and brought the apostles back. They did not use force, however, because they were afraid that the people might stone them.

²⁷They brought the apostles in, made them stand before the Council, and the High Priest questioned them. ²⁸"We gave you strict orders not to teach in the name of this man," he said; "but see what you have done! You have spread your teaching all over Jerusalem, and you want to make us responsible for his death!"

²⁹Peter and the other apostles replied, "We must obey God, not men. ³⁰The God of our ancestors raised Jesus from death, after you had killed him by nailing him to a cross. ³¹God raised him to his right-hand side as Leader and Saviour, to give the people of Israel the opportunity to repent and have their sins forgiven. ³²We are witnesses to these things — we and the Holy Spirit, who is God's gift to those who obey him."

³³When the members of the Council heard this, they were so furious that they wanted to have the apostles put to death. ³⁴But one of them, a Pharisee named Gamaliel, who was a teacher of the Law and was highly respected by all the people, stood up in the Council. He ordered the apostles to be taken out for a while, ³⁵and then he said to the Council, "Fellow-Israelites, be careful what you do to these men. ³⁶You remember that Theudas appeared some time ago, claiming to be somebody great, and about 400 men joined him. But he was killed, all his followers were scattered, and his movement died out. ³⁷After

that, Judas the Galilean appeared during the time of the census; he drew a crowd after him, but he also was killed, and all his followers were scattered. [38] And so in this case, I tell you, do not take any action against these men. Leave them alone! If what they have planned and done is of human origin, it will disappear, [39] but if it comes from God, you cannot possibly defeat them. You could find yourselves fighting against God!"

The Council followed Gamaliel's advice. [40] They called the apostles in, had them whipped, and ordered them never again to speak in the name of Jesus; and then they set them free. [41] As the apostles left the Council, they were happy, because God had considered them worthy to suffer disgrace for the sake of Jesus. [42] And every day in the Temple and in people's homes they continued to teach and preach the Good News about Jesus the Messiah.

And crowds of people came in from the towns around Jerusalem, bringing those who were ill or who had evil spirits in them; and they were all healed.

Acts 5.16

Reflect

The community that followed Jesus gathered together to eat, pray, worship and serve the poor. At the heart of this community was the message of the life, death and resurrection of Jesus, and the experience of the power of the Holy Spirit in the lives of his followers.

The empowerment of God was not impractical. Even without Jesus physically there, he was still amongst them and healing through them, through the power of the Holy Spirit. That power, which went well beyond words, was making people whole and transforming the lives of the poor and sick. It was bringing reassurance, stability, health and wholeness – empowering all of them to be changed and to change others.

But this empowerment was grounded in reality – those who followed Jesus' teachings still faced hatred and threats to their lives. By being empowered, they were able to face these threats head on, to grow and thrive in the difficult times, and to continue to change the lives of those around them. Though Jesus may not physically be with us, he walks with us, and his power acts through us. Can you see the signs of that power at work in your own life and the lives of those around you?

Pray

Holy Spirit, the giver of strength,
bring wholeness to my life.
Help me to sense Jesus as he walks with me through my life.
Through that wholeness and closeness to Jesus,
empower me in all I say
and all I do in God's service.
Amen

Act

There are things that give us power every day – food, books,
friendship, even power chargers and light switches. Think of
something that gives you power in some way. Every time you
use it or spend time with it during the day, let it remind you to
ask for more of God's power in your own life.

The Seven Helpers

[1] Some time later, as the number of disciples kept growing, there was a quarrel between the Greek-speaking Jews and the native Jews. The Greek-speaking Jews claimed that their widows were being neglected in the daily distribution of funds. [2] So the twelve apostles called the whole group of believers together and said, "It is not right for us to neglect the preaching of God's word in order to handle finances. [3] So then, brothers and sisters, choose seven men among you who are known to be full of the Holy Spirit and wisdom, and we will put them in charge of this matter. [4] We ourselves, then, will give our full time to prayer and the work of preaching."

[5] The whole group was pleased with the apostles' proposal, so they chose Stephen, a man full of faith and the Holy Spirit, and Philip, Prochorus, Nicanor, Timon, Parmenas, and Nicolaus, a Gentile from Antioch who had earlier been converted to Judaism. [6] The group presented them to the apostles, who prayed and placed their hands on them.

[7] And so the word of God continued to spread. The number of disciples in Jerusalem grew larger and larger, and a great number of priests accepted the faith.

The Arrest of Stephen

[8] Stephen, a man richly blessed by God and full of power, performed great miracles and wonders among the people. [9] But he was opposed by some men who were members of the synagogue of the Freedmen (as it was called), which included Jews from Cyrene and Alexandria. They and other Jews from the provinces of Cilicia and Asia started arguing with Stephen. [10] But the Spirit gave Stephen such wisdom that when he spoke, they could not refute him. [11] So they bribed some men to say, "We heard him speaking against Moses and against God!" [12] In this way they stirred up the people, the elders, and the teachers of the Law. They seized Stephen and took him before the Council. [13] Then they brought in some men to tell lies about him. "This man," they said, "is always talking against our sacred Temple and the Law of Moses. [14] We heard him say that this Jesus of Nazareth will tear down the Temple and change all the customs which have come down to us from Moses!" [15] All those sitting in the Council fixed their eyes on Stephen and saw that his face looked like the face of an angel.

Stephen's Speech

[1] The High Priest asked Stephen, "Is this true?"

[2] Stephen answered, "Brothers and fathers, listen to me! Before our ancestor Abraham had gone to live in Haran, the God of glory appeared to him in Mesopotamia [3] and said to him, 'Leave your family and country and go to the land that I will show you.' [4] And so he left his country and went to live in Haran. After Abraham's father died, God made him move to this land where you now live. [5] God did not then give Abraham any part of it as his own, not even a square metre of ground, but God promised to give it to him, and that it would belong to him and to his descendants. At the time God made this promise, Abraham had no children. [6] This is what God said to him: 'Your descendants will live in a foreign country, where they will be slaves and will be badly treated for 400 years. [7] But I will pass judgement on the people that they will serve, and afterwards your descendants will come out of that country and will worship me in this place.' [8] Then God gave Abraham the ceremony of circumcision as a sign of the covenant. So Abraham circumcised Isaac a week after he was born; Isaac circumcised his son Jacob, and Jacob circumcised his twelve sons, the famous ancestors of our race.

[9] "Jacob's sons became jealous of their brother Joseph and sold him to be a slave in Egypt. But God was with him [10] and brought him safely through all his troubles. When Joseph appeared before the king of Egypt, God gave him a pleasing manner and wisdom, and the king made Joseph governor over the country and the royal household. [11] Then there was a famine all over Egypt and Canaan, which caused much suffering. Our ancestors could not find any food, [12] and when Jacob heard that there was corn in Egypt, he sent his sons, our ancestors, on their first visit there. [13] On the second visit Joseph made himself known to his brothers, and the king of Egypt came to know about Joseph's family. [14] So Joseph sent a message to his father Jacob, telling him and the whole family, 75 people in all, to come to Egypt. [15] Then Jacob went to Egypt, where he and his sons died. [16] Their bodies were taken to Shechem, where they were buried in the grave which Abraham had bought from the clan of Hamor for a sum of money.

[17] "When the time drew near for God to keep the promise he had made to Abraham, the number of our people in Egypt had grown much larger. [18] At last a king who did not know about Joseph began to rule in Egypt. [19] He tricked our ancestors and was cruel to them, forcing them to put their babies out of their homes, so that they would die. [20] It was

at this time that Moses was born, a very beautiful child. He was cared for at home for three months, [21] and when he was put out of his home, the king's daughter adopted him and brought him up as her own son. [22] He was taught all the wisdom of the Egyptians and became a great man in words and deeds.

[23] "When Moses was forty years old, he decided to find out how his fellow-Israelites were being treated. [24] He saw one of them being ill-treated by an Egyptian, so he went to his help and took revenge on the Egyptian by killing him. [25] (He thought that his own people would understand that God was going to use him to set them free, but they did not understand.) [26] The next day he saw two Israelites fighting, and he tried to make peace between them. 'Listen, men,' he said, 'you are fellow-Israelites; why are you fighting like this?' [27] But the one who was ill-treating the other pushed Moses aside. 'Who made you ruler and judge over us?' he asked. [28] 'Do you want to kill me, just as you killed that Egyptian yesterday?' [29] When Moses heard this, he fled from Egypt and went to live in the land of Midian. There he had two sons.

[30] "After forty years had passed, an angel appeared to Moses in the flames of a burning bush in the desert near Mount Sinai. [31] Moses was amazed by what he saw, and went near the bush to get a better look. But he heard the Lord's voice: [32] 'I am the God of your ancestors, the God of Abraham, Isaac, and Jacob.' Moses trembled with fear and dared not look. [33] The Lord said to him, 'Take your sandals off, for the place where you are standing is holy ground. [34] I have seen the cruel suffering of my people in Egypt. I have heard their groans, and I have come down to set them free. Come now; I will send you to Egypt.'

[35] "Moses is the one who was rejected by the people of Israel. 'Who made you ruler and judge over us?' they asked. He is the one whom God sent to rule the people and set them free with the help of the angel who appeared to him in the burning bush. [36] He led the people out of Egypt, performing miracles and wonders in Egypt and at the Red Sea and for forty years in the desert. [37] Moses is the one who said to the people of Israel, 'God will send you a prophet, just as he sent me, and he will be one of your own people.' [38] He is the one who was with the people of Israel assembled in the desert; he was there with our ancestors and with the angel who spoke to him on Mount Sinai, and he received God's living messages to pass on to us.

[39] "But our ancestors refused to obey him; they pushed him aside and wished that they could go back to Egypt. [40] So they said to Aaron, 'Make us some gods who will lead us. We do not know what has

happened to that man Moses, who brought us out of Egypt.' [41] It was then that they made an idol in the shape of a bull, offered sacrifice to it, and had a feast in honour of what they themselves had made. [42] So God turned away from them and gave them over to worship the stars of heaven, as it is written in the book of the prophets:

> 'People of Israel! It was not to me
> > that you slaughtered and sacrificed animals
> > for forty years in the desert.
> [43] It was the tent of the god Molech that you carried,
> > and the image of Rephan, your star god;
> > they were idols that you had made to worship.
> And so I will send you into exile beyond Babylon.'

[44] "Our ancestors had the Tent of God's presence with them in the desert. It had been made as God had told Moses to make it, according to the pattern that Moses had been shown. [45] Later on, our ancestors who received the tent from their fathers carried it with them when they went with Joshua and took over the land from the nations that God drove out as they advanced. And it stayed there until the time of David. [46] He won God's favour and asked God to allow him to provide a dwelling place for the God of Jacob. [47] But it was Solomon who built him a house.

[48] "But the Most High God does not live in houses built by human hands; as the prophet says:

> [49] 'Heaven is my throne, says the Lord,
> > and the earth is my footstool.
> What kind of house would you build for me?
> > Where is the place for me to live in?
> [50] Did not I myself make all these things?'

[51] "How stubborn you are!" Stephen went on to say. "How heathen your hearts, how deaf you are to God's message! You are just like your ancestors: you too have always resisted the Holy Spirit! [52] Was there any prophet that your ancestors did not persecute? They killed God's messengers, who long ago announced the coming of his righteous Servant. And now you have betrayed and murdered him. [53] You are the ones who received God's law, that was handed down by angels — yet you have not obeyed it!"

The Stoning of Stephen

[54] As the members of the Council listened to Stephen, they became furious and ground their teeth at him in anger. [55] But Stephen, full of

the Holy Spirit, looked up to heaven and saw God's glory and Jesus standing at the right-hand side of God. [56] "Look!" he said. "I see heaven opened and the Son of Man standing at the right-hand side of God!"

[57] With a loud cry the members of the Council covered their ears with their hands. Then they all rushed at him at once, [58] threw him out of the city, and stoned him. The witnesses left their cloaks in the care of a young man named Saul. [59] They kept on stoning Stephen as he called out to the Lord, "Lord Jesus, receive my spirit!" [60] He knelt down and cried out in a loud voice, "Lord! Do not remember this sin against them!" He said this and died.

[1] And Saul approved of his murder.

Saul Persecutes the Church

That very day the church in Jerusalem began to suffer cruel persecution. All the believers, except the apostles, were scattered throughout the provinces of Judea and Samaria. [2] Some devout men buried Stephen, mourning for him with loud cries.

[3] But Saul tried to destroy the church; going from house to house, he dragged out the believers, both men and women, and threw them into jail.

The Gospel is Preached in Samaria

[4] The believers who were scattered went everywhere, preaching the message. [5] Philip went to the principal city in Samaria and preached the Messiah to the people there. [6] The crowds paid close attention to what Philip said, as they listened to him and saw the miracles that he performed. [7] Evil spirits came out from many people with a loud cry, and many paralysed and lame people were healed. [8] So there was great joy in that city.

[9] A man named Simon lived there, who for some time had astounded the Samaritans with his magic. He claimed that he was someone great, [10] and everyone in the city, from all classes of society, paid close attention to him. "He is that power of God known as 'The Great Power'," they said. [11] They paid this attention to him because for such a long time he had astonished them with his magic. [12] But when they believed Philip's message about the good news of the Kingdom of God and about Jesus Christ, they were baptized, both men and women. [13] Simon himself also believed; and after being baptized, he stayed close to Philip and was astounded when he saw the great wonders and miracles that were being performed.

[14] The apostles in Jerusalem heard that the people of Samaria had received the word of God, so they sent Peter and John to them. [15] When they arrived, they prayed for the believers that they might receive the Holy Spirit. [16] For the Holy Spirit had not yet come down on any of them; they had only been baptized in the name of the Lord Jesus. [17] Then Peter and John placed their hands on them, and they received the Holy Spirit.

[18] Simon saw that the Spirit had been given to the believers when the apostles placed their hands on them. So he offered money to Peter

and John, [19] and said, "Give this power to me too, so that anyone I place my hands on will receive the Holy Spirit."

[20] But Peter answered him, "May you and your money go to hell, for thinking that you can buy God's gift with money! [21] You have no part or share in our work, because your heart is not right in God's sight. [22] Repent, then, of this evil plan of yours, and pray to the Lord that he will forgive you for thinking such a thing as this. [23] For I see that you are full of bitter envy and are a prisoner of sin."

[24] Simon said to Peter and John, "Please pray to the Lord for me, so that none of these things you spoke of will happen to me."

[25] After they had given their testimony and proclaimed the Lord's message, Peter and John went back to Jerusalem. On their way they preached the Good News in many villages of Samaria.

Philip and the Ethiopian Official

[26] An angel of the Lord said to Philip, "Get ready and go south to the road that goes from Jerusalem to Gaza." (This road is not used nowadays.) [27-28] So Philip got ready and went. Now an Ethiopian eunuch, who was an important official in charge of the treasury of the queen of Ethiopia, was on his way home. He had been to Jerusalem to worship God and was going back home in his carriage. As he rode along, he was reading from the book of the prophet Isaiah. [29] The Holy Spirit said to Philip, "Go over to that carriage and stay close to it." [30] Philip ran over and heard him reading from the book of the prophet Isaiah. He asked him, "Do you understand what you are reading?"

[31] The official replied, "How can I understand unless someone explains it to me?" And he invited Philip to climb up and sit in the carriage with him. [32] The passage of scripture which he was reading was this:

> "Like a sheep that is taken to be slaughtered,
>> like a lamb that makes no sound when its wool is cut off,
>> he did not say a word.
> [33] He was humiliated, and justice was denied him.
>> No one will be able to tell about his descendants,
>> because his life on earth has come to an end."

[34] The official asked Philip, "Tell me, of whom is the prophet saying this? Of himself or of someone else?" [35] Then Philip began to speak; starting from this passage of scripture, he told him the Good News about Jesus. [36] As they travelled down the road, they came to a place

where there was some water, and the official said, "Here is some water. What is to keep me from being baptized?"

38 The official ordered the carriage to stop, and both Philip and the official went down into the water, and Philip baptized him. 39 When they came up out of the water, the Spirit of the Lord took Philip away. The official did not see him again, but continued on his way, full of joy. 40 Philip found himself in Azotus; he went on to Caesarea, and on the way he preached the Good News in every town.

The Conversion of Saul

[1] In the meantime Saul kept up his violent threats of murder against the followers of the Lord. He went to the High Priest [2] and asked for letters of introduction to the synagogues in Damascus, so that if he should find there any followers of the Way of the Lord, he would be able to arrest them, both men and women, and bring them back to Jerusalem.

[3] As Saul was coming near the city of Damascus, suddenly a light from the sky flashed round him. [4] He fell to the ground and heard a voice saying to him, "Saul, Saul! Why do you persecute me?"

[5] "Who are you, Lord?" he asked.

"I am Jesus, whom you persecute," the voice said. [6] "But get up and go into the city, where you will be told what you must do."

[7] The men who were travelling with Saul had stopped, not saying a word; they heard the voice but could not see anyone. [8] Saul got up from the ground and opened his eyes, but could not see a thing. So they took him by the hand and led him into Damascus. [9] For three days he was not able to see, and during that time he did not eat or drink anything.

[10] There was a believer in Damascus named Ananias. He had a vision, in which the Lord said to him, "Ananias!"

"Here I am, Lord," he answered.

[11] The Lord said to him, "Get ready and go to Straight Street, and at the house of Judas ask for a man from Tarsus named Saul. He is praying, [12] and in a vision he has seen a man named Ananias come in and place his hands on him so that he might see again."

[13] Ananias answered, "Lord, many people have told me about this man and about all the terrible things he has done to your people in Jerusalem. [14] And he has come to Damascus with authority from the chief priests to arrest all who worship you."

[15] The Lord said to him, "Go, because I have chosen him to serve me, to make my name known to Gentiles and kings and to the people of Israel. [16] And I myself will show him all that he must suffer for my sake."

[17] So Ananias went, entered the house where Saul was, and placed his hands on him. "Brother Saul," he said, "the Lord has sent me — Jesus himself, who appeared to you on the road as you were coming here. He sent me so that you might see again and be filled with the Holy Spirit."

¹⁸ At once something like fish scales fell from Saul's eyes, and he was able to see again. He stood up and was baptized; ¹⁹ and after he had eaten, his strength came back.

Saul Preaches in Damascus

Saul stayed for a few days with the believers in Damascus. ²⁰ He went straight to the synagogues and began to preach that Jesus was the Son of God.

²¹ All who heard him were amazed and asked, "Isn't he the one who in Jerusalem was killing those who worship that man Jesus? And didn't he come here for the very purpose of arresting those people and taking them back to the chief priests?"

²² But Saul's preaching became even more powerful, and his proofs that Jesus was the Messiah were so convincing that the Jews who lived in Damascus could not answer him.

²³ After many days had gone by, the Jews met together and made plans to kill Saul, ²⁴ but he was told of their plan. Day and night they watched the city gates in order to kill him. ²⁵ But one night Saul's followers took him and let him down through an opening in the wall, lowering him in a basket.

Saul in Jerusalem

²⁶ Saul went to Jerusalem and tried to join the disciples. But they would not believe that he was a disciple, and they were all afraid of him. ²⁷ Then Barnabas came to his help and took him to the apostles. He explained to them how Saul had seen the Lord on the road and that the Lord had spoken to him. He also told them how boldly Saul had preached in the name of Jesus in Damascus. ²⁸ And so Saul stayed with them and went all over Jerusalem, preaching boldly in the name of the Lord. ²⁹ He also talked and disputed with the Greek-speaking Jews, but they tried to kill him. ³⁰ When the believers found out about this, they took Saul to Caesarea and sent him away to Tarsus.

³¹ And so it was that the church throughout Judea, Galilee, and Samaria had a time of peace. Through the help of the Holy Spirit it was strengthened and grew in numbers, as it lived in reverence for the Lord.

Peter in Lydda and Joppa

³² Peter travelled everywhere, and on one occasion he went to visit God's people who lived in Lydda. ³³ There he met a man named

Aeneas, who was paralysed and had not been able to get out of bed for eight years. [34] "Aeneas," Peter said to him, "Jesus Christ makes you well. Get up and make your bed." At once Aeneas got up. [35] All the people living in Lydda and Sharon saw him, and they turned to the Lord.

[36] In Joppa there was a woman named Tabitha, who was a believer. (Her name in Greek is Dorcas, meaning "a deer".) She spent all her time doing good and helping the poor. [37] At that time she became ill and died. Her body was washed and laid in a room upstairs. [38] Joppa was not very far from Lydda, and when the believers in Joppa heard that Peter was in Lydda, they sent two men to him with the message, "Please hurry and come to us." [39] So Peter got ready and went with them. When he arrived, he was taken to the room upstairs, where all the widows crowded round him, crying and showing him all the shirts and coats that Dorcas had made while she was alive. [40] Peter put them all out of the room, and knelt down and prayed; then he turned to the body and said, "Tabitha, get up!" She opened her eyes, and when she saw Peter, she sat up. [41] Peter reached over and helped her get up. Then he called all the believers, including the widows, and presented her alive to them. [42] The news about this spread all over Joppa, and many people believed in the Lord. [43] Peter stayed on in Joppa for many days with a tanner of leather named Simon.

Peter and Cornelius

[1] There was a man in Caesarea named Cornelius, who was a captain in the Roman regiment called "The Italian Regiment". [2] He was a religious man; he and his whole family worshipped God. He also did much to help the Jewish poor people and was constantly praying to God. [3] It was about three o'clock one afternoon when he had a vision, in which he clearly saw an angel of God come in and say to him, "Cornelius!"

[4] He stared at the angel in fear and said, "What is it, sir?"

The angel answered, "God is pleased with your prayers and works of charity, and is ready to answer you. [5] And now send some men to Joppa for a certain man whose full name is Simon Peter. [6] He is a guest in the home of a tanner of leather named Simon, who lives by the sea." [7] Then the angel went away, and Cornelius called two of his house servants and a soldier, a religious man who was one of his personal attendants. [8] He told them what had happened and sent them off to Joppa.

[9] The next day, as they were on their way and coming near Joppa, Peter went up on the roof of the house about noon in order to pray. [10] He became hungry and wanted something to eat; while the food was being prepared, he had a vision. [11] He saw heaven opened and something coming down that looked like a large sheet being lowered by its four corners to the earth. [12] In it were all kinds of animals, reptiles, and wild birds. [13] A voice said to him, "Get up, Peter; kill and eat!"

[14] But Peter said, "Certainly not, Lord! I have never eaten anything ritually unclean or defiled."

[15] The voice spoke to him again, "Do not consider anything unclean that God has declared clean." [16] This happened three times, and then the thing was taken back up into heaven.

[17] While Peter was wondering about the meaning of this vision, the men sent by Cornelius had learnt where Simon's house was, and they were now standing in front of the gate. [18] They called out and asked, "Is there a guest here by the name of Simon Peter?"

[19] Peter was still trying to understand what the vision meant, when the Spirit said, "Listen! Three men are here looking for you. [20] So get ready and go down, and do not hesitate to go with them, for I have sent them." [21] So Peter went down and said to the men, "I am the man you are looking for. Why have you come?"

22 "Captain Cornelius sent us," they answered. "He is a good man who worships God and is highly respected by all the Jewish people. An angel of God told him to invite you to his house, so that he could hear what you have to say." 23 Peter invited the men in and persuaded them to spend the night there.

The next day he got ready and went with them; and some of the believers from Joppa went along with him. 24 The following day he arrived in Caesarea, where Cornelius was waiting for him, together with relatives and close friends that he had invited. 25 As Peter was about to go in, Cornelius met him, fell at his feet, and bowed down before him. 26 But Peter made him rise. "Stand up," he said; "I myself am only a man." 27 Peter kept on talking to Cornelius as he went into the house, where he found many people gathered. 28 He said to them, "You yourselves know very well that a Jew is not allowed by his religion to visit or associate with Gentiles. But God has shown me that I must not consider any person ritually unclean or defiled. 29 And so when you sent for me, I came without any objection. I ask you, then, why did you send for me?"

30 Cornelius said, "It was about this time three days ago that I was praying in my house at three o'clock in the afternoon. Suddenly a man dressed in shining clothes stood in front of me 31 and said: 'Cornelius! God has heard your prayer and has taken notice of your works of charity. 32 Send someone to Joppa for a man whose full name is Simon Peter. He is a guest in the home of Simon the tanner of leather, who lives by the sea.' 33 And so I sent for you at once, and you have been good enough to come. Now we are all here in the presence of God, waiting to hear anything that the Lord has instructed you to say."

Peter's Speech

34 Peter began to speak: "I now realize that it is true that God treats everyone on the same basis. 35 Those who worship him and do what is right are acceptable to him, no matter what race they belong to. 36 You know the message he sent to the people of Israel, proclaiming the Good News of peace through Jesus Christ, who is Lord of all. 37 You know of the great event that took place throughout the land of Israel, beginning in Galilee after John preached his message of baptism. 38 You know about Jesus of Nazareth and how God poured out on him the Holy Spirit and power. He went everywhere, doing good and healing all who were under the power of the Devil, for God was with him. 39 We are witnesses of everything that he did in the land of

Israel and in Jerusalem. Then they put him to death by nailing him to a cross. [40] But God raised him from death three days later and caused him to appear, [41] not to everyone, but only to the witnesses that God had already chosen, that is, to us who ate and drank with him after he rose from death. [42] And he commanded us to preach the gospel to the people and to testify that he is the one whom God has appointed judge of the living and the dead. [43] All the prophets spoke about him, saying that all who believe in him will have their sins forgiven through the power of his name."

The Gentiles Receive the Holy Spirit

[44] While Peter was still speaking, the Holy Spirit came down on all those who were listening to his message. [45] The Jewish believers who had come from Joppa with Peter were amazed that God had poured out his gift of the Holy Spirit on the Gentiles also. [46] For they heard them speaking in strange tongues and praising God's greatness. Peter spoke up: [47] "These people have received the Holy Spirit, just as we also did. Can anyone, then, stop them from being baptized with water?" [48] So he ordered them to be baptized in the name of Jesus Christ. Then they asked him to stay with them for a few days.

Peter's Report to the Church at Jerusalem

[1] The apostles and the other believers throughout Judea heard that the Gentiles also had received the word of God. [2] When Peter went to Jerusalem, those who were in favour of circumcising Gentiles criticized him, saying, [3] "You were a guest in the home of uncircumcised Gentiles, and you even ate with them!" [4] So Peter gave them a complete account of what had happened from the very beginning:

[5] "While I was praying in the city of Joppa, I had a vision. I saw something coming down that looked like a large sheet being lowered by its four corners from heaven, and it stopped next to me. [6] I looked closely inside and saw domesticated and wild animals, reptiles, and wild birds. [7] Then I heard a voice saying to me, 'Get up, Peter; kill and eat!' [8] But I said, 'Certainly not, Lord! No ritually unclean or defiled food has ever entered my mouth.' [9] The voice spoke again from heaven, 'Do not consider anything unclean that God has declared clean.' [10] This happened three times, and finally the whole thing was drawn back up into heaven. [11] At that very moment three men who had been sent to me from Caesarea arrived at the house where I was staying. [12] The Spirit told me to go with them without hesitation. These six fellow-believers from Joppa accompanied me to Caesarea, and we all went into the house of Cornelius. [13] He told us how he had seen an angel standing in his house, who said to him, 'Send someone to Joppa for a man whose full name is Simon Peter. [14] He will speak words to you by which you and all your family will be saved.' [15] And when I began to speak, the Holy Spirit came down on them just as on us at the beginning. [16] Then I remembered what the Lord had said: 'John baptized with water, but you will be baptized with the Holy Spirit.' [17] It is clear that God gave those Gentiles the same gift that he gave us when we believed in the Lord Jesus Christ; who was I, then, to try to stop God!"

[18] When they heard this, they stopped their criticism and praised God, saying, "Then God has given to the Gentiles also the opportunity to repent and live!"

The Church at Antioch

[19] Some of the believers who were scattered by the persecution which took place when Stephen was killed went as far as Phoenicia, Cyprus, and Antioch, telling the message to Jews only. [20] But other believers, who were from Cyprus and Cyrene, went to Antioch and proclaimed the message to Gentiles also, telling them the Good News about the

Lord Jesus. [21] The Lord's power was with them, and a great number of people believed and turned to the Lord.

[22] The news about this reached the church in Jerusalem, so they sent Barnabas to Antioch. [23] When he arrived and saw how God had blessed the people, he was glad and urged them all to be faithful and true to the Lord with all their hearts. [24] Barnabas was a good man, full of the Holy Spirit and faith, and many people were brought to the Lord.

[25] Then Barnabas went to Tarsus to look for Saul. [26] When he found him, he took him to Antioch, and for a whole year the two met with the people of the church and taught a large group. It was at Antioch that the believers were first called Christians.

[27] About that time some prophets went from Jerusalem to Antioch. [28] One of them, named Agabus, stood up and by the power of the Spirit predicted that a severe famine was about to come over all the earth. (It came when Claudius was emperor.) [29] The disciples decided that they would each send as much as they could to help their fellow-believers who lived in Judea. [30] They did this, then, and sent the money to the church elders by Barnabas and Saul.

More Persecution

[1] About this time King Herod began to persecute some members of the church. [2] He had James, the brother of John, put to death by the sword. [3] When he saw that this pleased the Jews, he went on to arrest Peter. (This happened during the time of the Festival of Unleavened Bread.) [4] After his arrest Peter was put in jail, where he was handed over to be guarded by four groups of four soldiers each. Herod planned to put him on trial in public after Passover. [5] So Peter was kept in jail, but the people of the church were praying earnestly to God for him.

Peter is Set Free from Prison

[6] The night before Herod was going to bring him out to the people, Peter was sleeping between two guards. He was tied with two chains, and there were guards on duty at the prison gate. [7] Suddenly an angel of the Lord stood there, and a light shone in the cell. The angel shook Peter by the shoulder, woke him up, and said, "Hurry! Get up!" At once the chains fell off Peter's hands. [8] Then the angel said, "Fasten your belt and put on your sandals." Peter did so, and the angel said, "Put your cloak round you and come with me." [9] Peter followed him out of the prison, not knowing, however, if what the angel was doing was real; he thought he was seeing a vision. [10] They passed by the first guard post and then the second, and came at last to the iron gate leading into the city. The gate opened for them by itself, and they went out. They walked down a street, and suddenly the angel left Peter.

[11] Then Peter realized what had happened to him, and said, "Now I know that it is really true! The Lord sent his angel to rescue me from Herod's power and from everything the Jewish people expected to happen."

[12] Aware of his situation, he went to the home of Mary, the mother of John Mark, where many people had gathered and were praying. [13] Peter knocked at the outside door, and a servant named Rhoda came to answer it. [14] She recognized Peter's voice and was so happy that she ran back in without opening the door, and announced that Peter was standing outside. [15] "You are mad!" they told her. But she insisted that it was true. So they answered, "It is his angel."

[16] Meanwhile Peter kept on knocking. At last they opened the door, and when they saw him, they were amazed. [17] He motioned with his hand for them to be quiet, and he explained to them how the Lord had brought him out of prison. "Tell this to James and the rest of the believers," he said; then he left and went somewhere else.

[18] When morning came, there was a tremendous confusion among the guards — what had happened to Peter? [19] Herod gave orders to search for him, but they could not find him. So he had the guards questioned and ordered them to be put to death.

After this, Herod left Judea and spent some time in Caesarea.

The Death of Herod

[20] Herod was very angry with the people of Tyre and Sidon, so they went in a group to see him. First they convinced Blastus, the man in charge of the palace, that he should help them. Then they went to Herod and asked him for peace, because their country got its food supplies from the king's country.

[21] On a chosen day Herod put on his royal robes, sat on his throne, and made a speech to the people. [22] "It isn't a man speaking, but a god!" they shouted. [23] At once the angel of the Lord struck Herod down, because he did not give honour to God. He was eaten by worms and died.

[24] Meanwhile the word of God continued to spread and grow.

[25] Barnabas and Saul finished their mission and returned from Jerusalem, taking John Mark with them.

Barnabas and Saul are Chosen and Sent

[1] In the church at Antioch there were some prophets and teachers: Barnabas, Simeon (called the Black), Lucius (from Cyrene), Manaen (who had been brought up with Herod the governor), and Saul. [2] While they were serving the Lord and fasting, the Holy Spirit said to them, "Set apart for me Barnabas and Saul, to do the work to which I have called them."

[3] They fasted and prayed, placed their hands on them, and sent them off.

In Cyprus

[4] Having been sent by the Holy Spirit, Barnabas and Saul went to Seleucia and sailed from there to the island of Cyprus. [5] When they arrived at Salamis, they preached the word of God in the synagogues. They had John Mark with them to help in the work.

[6] They went all the way across the island to Paphos, where they met a certain magician named Bar-Jesus, a Jew who claimed to be a prophet. [7] He was a friend of the governor of the island, Sergius Paulus, who was an intelligent man. The governor called Barnabas and Saul before him because he wanted to hear the word of God. [8] But they were opposed by the magician Elymas (that is his name in Greek), who tried to turn the governor away from the faith. [9] Then Saul — also known as Paul — was filled with the Holy Spirit; he looked straight at the magician [10] and said, "You son of the Devil! You are the enemy of everything that is good. You are full of all kinds of evil tricks, and you always keep trying to turn the Lord's truths into lies! [11] The Lord's hand will come down on you now; you will be blind and will not see the light of day for a time."

At once Elymas felt a dark mist cover his eyes, and he walked about trying to find someone to lead him by the hand. [12] When the governor saw what had happened, he believed; for he was greatly amazed at the teaching about the Lord.

In Antioch in Pisidia

[13] Paul and his companions sailed from Paphos and came to Perga, a city in Pamphylia, where John Mark left them and went back to Jerusalem. [14] They went on from Perga and arrived in Antioch in Pisidia, and on the Sabbath they went into the synagogue and sat down. [15] After the reading from the Law of Moses and from the

writings of the prophets, the officials of the synagogue sent them a message: "Brothers and sisters, we want you to speak to the people if you have a message of encouragement for them." [16] Paul stood up, motioned with his hand, and began to speak:

"Fellow-Israelites and all Gentiles here who worship God: hear me! [17] The God of the people of Israel chose our ancestors and made the people a great nation during the time they lived as foreigners in Egypt. God brought them out of Egypt by his great power, [18] and for forty years he endured them in the desert. [19] He destroyed seven nations in the land of Canaan and made his people the owners of the land. [20] All this took about 450 years.

"After this he gave them judges until the time of the prophet Samuel. [21] And when they asked for a king, God gave them Saul son of Kish from the tribe of Benjamin, to be their king for forty years. [22] After removing him, God made David their king. This is what God said about him: 'I have found that David son of Jesse is the kind of man I like, a man who will do all I want him to do.' [23] It was Jesus, a descendant of David, whom God made the Saviour of the people of Israel, as he had promised. [24] Before Jesus began his work, John preached to all the people of Israel that they should turn from their sins and be baptized. [25] And as John was about to finish his mission, he said to the people, 'Who do you think I am? I am not the one you are waiting for. But listen! He is coming after me, and I am not good enough to take his sandals off his feet.'

[26] "My fellow-Israelites, descendants of Abraham, and all Gentiles here who worship God: it is to us that this message of salvation has been sent! [27] For the people who live in Jerusalem and their leaders did not know that he is the Saviour, nor did they understand the words of the prophets that are read every Sabbath. Yet they made the prophets' words come true by condemning Jesus. [28] And even though they could find no reason to pass the death sentence on him, they asked Pilate to have him put to death. [29] And after they had done everything that the Scriptures say about him, they took him down from the cross and placed him in a tomb. [30] But God raised him from death, [31] and for many days he appeared to those who had travelled with him from Galilee to Jerusalem. They are now witnesses for him to the people of Israel. [32-33] And we are here to bring the Good News to you: what God promised our ancestors he would do, he has now done for us, who are their descendants, by raising Jesus to life. As it is written in the second Psalm:

> 'You are my Son;
> today I have become your Father.'

³⁴ And this is what God said about raising him from death, never to rot away in the grave:

> 'I will give you the sacred and sure blessings
> that I promised to David.'

³⁵ As indeed he says in another passage:

> 'You will not allow your faithful servant to rot in the grave.'

³⁶ For David served God's purposes in his own time, and then he died, was buried with his ancestors, and his body rotted in the grave. ³⁷ But this did not happen to the one whom God raised from death. ³⁸⁻³⁹ We want you to know, my fellow-Israelites, that it is through Jesus that the message about forgiveness of sins is preached to you; and that everyone who believes in him is set free from all the sins from which the Law of Moses could not set you free. ⁴⁰ Take care, then, so that what the prophets said may not happen to you:

> ⁴¹ 'Look, you scoffers! Be astonished and die!
> For what I am doing today
> is something that you will not believe,
> even when someone explains it to you!'"

⁴² As Paul and Barnabas were leaving the synagogue, the people invited them to come back the next Sabbath and tell them more about these things. ⁴³ After the people had left the meeting, Paul and Barnabas were followed by many Jews and by many Gentiles who had been converted to Judaism. The apostles spoke to them and encouraged them to keep on living in the grace of God.

⁴⁴ The next Sabbath nearly everyone in the town came to hear the word of the Lord. ⁴⁵ When the Jews saw the crowds, they were filled with jealousy; they disputed what Paul was saying and insulted him. ⁴⁶ But Paul and Barnabas spoke out even more boldly: "It was necessary that the word of God should be spoken first to you. But since you reject it and do not consider yourselves worthy of eternal life, we will leave you and go to the Gentiles. ⁴⁷ For this is the commandment that the Lord has given us:

> 'I have made you a light for the Gentiles,
> so that all the world may be saved.'"

⁴⁸ When the Gentiles heard this, they were glad and praised the Lord's message; and those who had been chosen for eternal life became believers.

[49] The word of the Lord spread everywhere in that region. [50] But the Jews stirred up the leading men of the city and the Gentile women of high social standing who worshipped God. They started a persecution against Paul and Barnabas and threw them out of their region. [51] The apostles shook the dust off their feet in protest against them and went on to Iconium. [52] The believers in Antioch were full of joy and the Holy Spirit.

In Iconium

[1] The same thing happened in Iconium: Paul and Barnabas went to the synagogue and spoke in such a way that a great number of Jews and Gentiles became believers. [2] But the Jews who would not believe stirred up the Gentiles and turned them against the believers. [3] The apostles stayed there for a long time, speaking boldly about the Lord, who proved that their message about his grace was true by giving them the power to perform miracles and wonders. [4] The people of the city were divided: some were for the Jews, others for the apostles.

[5] Then some Gentiles and Jews, together with their leaders, decided to ill-treat the apostles and stone them. [6] When the apostles learnt about it, they fled to the cities of Lystra and Derbe in Lycaonia and to the surrounding territory. [7] There they preached the Good News.

In Lystra and Derbe

[8] In Lystra there was a man who had been lame from birth and had never been able to walk. [9] He sat there and listened to Paul's words. Paul saw that he believed and could be healed, so he looked straight at him [10] and said in a loud voice, "Stand up straight on your feet!" The man jumped up and started walking around. [11] When the crowds saw what Paul had done, they started shouting in their own Lycaonian language, "The gods have become like men and have come down to us!" [12] They gave Barnabas the name Zeus, and Paul the name Hermes, because he was the chief speaker. [13] The priest of the god Zeus, whose temple stood just outside the town, brought bulls and flowers to the gate, for he and the crowds wanted to offer sacrifice to the apostles.

[14] When Barnabas and Paul heard what they were about to do, they tore their clothes and ran into the middle of the crowd, shouting, [15] "Why are you doing this? We ourselves are only human beings like you! We are here to announce the Good News, to turn you away from these worthless things to the living God, who made heaven, earth, sea, and all that is in them. [16] In the past he allowed all people to go their own way. [17] But he has always given evidence of his existence by the good things he does: he gives you rain from heaven and crops at the right times; he gives you food and fills your hearts with happiness." [18] Even with these words the apostles could hardly keep the crowd from offering a sacrifice to them.

[19] Some Jews came from Antioch in Pisidia and from Iconium; they won the crowd over to their side, stoned Paul and dragged him out of the town, thinking that he was dead. [20] But when the believers gathered

round him, he got up and went back into the town. The next day he and Barnabas went to Derbe.

The Return to Antioch in Syria

[21] Paul and Barnabas preached the Good News in Derbe and won many disciples. Then they went back to Lystra, to Iconium, and on to Antioch in Pisidia. [22] They strengthened the believers and encouraged them to remain true to the faith. "We must pass through many troubles to enter the Kingdom of God," they taught. [23] In each church they appointed elders, and with prayers and fasting they commended them to the Lord, in whom they had put their trust.

[24] After going through the territory of Pisidia, they came to Pamphylia. [25] There they preached the message in Perga and then went to Attalia, [26] and from there they sailed back to Antioch, the place where they had been commended to the care of God's grace for the work they had now completed.

[27] When they arrived in Antioch, they gathered the people of the church together and told them about all that God had done with them and how he had opened the way for the Gentiles to believe. [28] And they stayed a long time there with the believers.

The Meeting at Jerusalem

[1] Some men came from Judea to Antioch and started teaching the believers, "You cannot be saved unless you are circumcised as the Law of Moses requires." [2] Paul and Barnabas got into a fierce argument with them about this, so it was decided that Paul and Barnabas and some of the others in Antioch should go to Jerusalem and see the apostles and elders about this matter.

[3] They were sent on their way by the church; and as they went through Phoenicia and Samaria, they reported how the Gentiles had turned to God; this news brought great joy to all the believers. [4] When they arrived in Jerusalem, they were welcomed by the church, the apostles, and the elders, to whom they told all that God had done through them. [5] But some of the believers who belonged to the party of the Pharisees stood up and said, "The Gentiles must be circumcised and told to obey the Law of Moses."

[6] The apostles and the elders met together to consider this question. [7] After a long debate Peter stood up and said, "My brothers and sisters, you know that a long time ago God chose me from among you to preach the Good News to the Gentiles, so that they could hear and believe. [8] And God, who knows the thoughts of everyone, showed his approval of the Gentiles by giving the Holy Spirit to them, just as he had to us. [9] He made no difference between us and them; he forgave their sins because they believed. [10] So then, why do you now want to put God to the test by laying a load on the backs of the believers which neither our ancestors nor we ourselves were able to carry? [11] No! We believe and are saved by the grace of the Lord Jesus, just as they are."

[12] The whole group was silent as they heard Barnabas and Paul report all the miracles and wonders that God had performed through them among the Gentiles. [13] When they had finished speaking, James spoke up: "Listen to me, my brothers and sisters! [14] Simon has just explained how God first showed his care for the Gentiles by taking from among them a people to belong to him. [15] The words of the prophets agree completely with this. As the scripture says:

[16] 'After this I will return, says the Lord,
  and restore the kingdom of David.
 I will rebuild its ruins and make it strong again.
[17] And so all the rest of the human race will come to me,
  all the Gentiles whom I have called to be my own.
[18] So says the Lord, who made this known long ago.'

[19] "It is my opinion," James went on, "that we should not trouble the Gentiles who are turning to God. [20] Instead, we should write a letter telling them not to eat any food that is ritually unclean because it has been offered to idols; to keep themselves from sexual immorality; and not to eat any animal that has been strangled, or any blood. [21] For the Law of Moses has been read for a very long time in the synagogues every Sabbath, and his words are preached in every town."

The Letter to the Gentile Believers

[22] Then the apostles and the elders, together with the whole church, decided to choose some men from the group and send them to Antioch with Paul and Barnabas. They chose two men who were highly respected by the believers, Judas, called Barsabbas, and Silas, [23] and they sent the following letter by them:

"We, the apostles and the elders, your brothers, send greetings to all our brothers of Gentile birth who live in Antioch, Syria, and Cilicia. [24] We have heard that some who went from our group have troubled and upset you by what they said; they had not, however, received any instruction from us. [25] And so we have met together and have all agreed to choose some messengers and send them to you. They will go with our dear friends Barnabas and Paul, [26] who have risked their lives in the service of our Lord Jesus Christ. [27] We send you, then, Judas and Silas, who will tell you in person the same things we are writing. [28] The Holy Spirit and we have agreed not to put any other burden on you besides these necessary rules: [29] eat no food that has been offered to idols; eat no blood; eat no animal that has been strangled; and keep yourselves from sexual immorality. You will do well if you take care not to do these things. With our best wishes."

[30] The messengers were sent off and went to Antioch, where they gathered the whole group of believers and gave them the letter. [31] When the people read it, they were filled with joy by the message of encouragement. [32] Judas and Silas, who were themselves prophets, spoke a long time with them, giving them courage and strength. [33] After spending some time there, they were sent off in peace by the believers and went back to those who had sent them.

[35] Paul and Barnabas spent some time in Antioch, and together with many others they taught and preached the word of the Lord.

Paul and Barnabas Separate

[36] Some time later Paul said to Barnabas, "Let us go back and visit our brothers and sisters in every town where we preached the word of the Lord, and let us find out how they are getting on." [37] Barnabas wanted to take John Mark with them, [38] but Paul did not think it was right to take him, because he had not stayed with them to the end of their mission, but had turned back and left them in Pamphylia. [39] There was a sharp argument, and they separated: Barnabas took Mark and sailed off for Cyprus, [40] while Paul chose Silas and left, commended by the believers to the care of the Lord's grace. [41] He went through Syria and Cilicia, strengthening the churches.

"He made no difference between
us and them; he forgave their sins
because they believed."

Reflect

Paul was not the natural choice to champion the cause of non-Jewish Christians, or Gentiles as they were called. He had spent so much time arresting and threatening new Christians, focusing on the barriers he believed separated those he thought were holy from those he thought weren't. He had caused harm and pain to new Christians.

Peter had also put up barriers. He originally thought that Gentiles were unclean, that they were excluded from God's kingdom, and that they couldn't receive the Holy Spirit in the same way Jews could.

But now both Paul and Peter had been challenged on their ideas about who was welcome to the family of God and who wasn't. Now they both saw that all were welcome as brothers and sisters in Jesus, the saviour of Jews and non-Jews alike. The barriers were gone, and they were part of a much larger family than they had realised. For them, the proof of the Gentiles' right to belong in the new Christian family was God giving the gift of the Holy Spirit to them too.

Just like Paul and Peter, we have barriers and phobias. There are people who make us feel uncomfortable, people we feel don't belong, people we wouldn't welcome in. Just like Paul and Peter, we need to challenge those barriers and break them down. And as Paul recognised the harm his barriers had caused, we need to see the harm our barriers have caused.

Without those barriers, who around you might be a surprising choice for you to welcome more deeply into your own life, prompted by the Holy Spirit?

Pray

Holy Spirit, who offers a welcome to all,
help me to follow the example of Peter and Paul.
Make me aware of the barriers I've built
against people I don't feel belong,
and strengthen me to break those barriers down.
Help me to grow in kindness
towards all those who are different from me,
and forgive me for when I have not been welcoming.
Amen

Act

Can you show a new act of kindness to someone around you every day? Someone you know, or someone you may not have welcomed before due to the barriers you'd built? This could be anything, from a compliment or an encouraging message, to getting someone a tea or coffee. How can you make your life much more welcoming to those around you?

Timothy Goes with Paul and Silas

[1] Paul travelled on to Derbe and Lystra, where a Christian named Timothy lived. His mother, who was also a Christian, was Jewish, but his father was a Greek. [2] All the believers in Lystra and Iconium spoke well of Timothy. [3] Paul wanted to take Timothy along with him, so he circumcised him. He did so because all the Jews who lived in those places knew that Timothy's father was Greek. [4] As they went through the towns, they delivered to the believers the rules decided upon by the apostles and elders in Jerusalem, and told them to obey those rules. [5] So the churches were made stronger in the faith and grew in numbers every day.

In Troas: Paul's Vision

[6] They travelled through the region of Phrygia and Galatia because the Holy Spirit did not let them preach the message in the province of Asia. [7] When they reached the border of Mysia, they tried to go into the province of Bithynia, but the Spirit of Jesus did not allow them. [8] So they travelled right on through Mysia and went to Troas. [9] That night Paul had a vision in which he saw a Macedonian standing and begging him, "Come over to Macedonia and help us!" [10] As soon as Paul had this vision, we got ready to leave for Macedonia, because we decided that God had called us to preach the Good News to the people there.

In Philippi: the Conversion of Lydia

[11] We left by ship from Troas and sailed straight across to Samothrace, and the next day to Neapolis. [12] From there we went inland to Philippi, a city of the first district of Macedonia; it is also a Roman colony. We spent several days there. [13] On the Sabbath we went out of the city to the riverside, where we thought there would be a place where Jews gathered for prayer. We sat down and talked to the women who gathered there. [14] One of those who heard us was Lydia from Thyatira, who was a dealer in purple cloth. She was a woman who worshipped God, and the Lord opened her mind to pay attention to what Paul was saying. [15] After she and the people of her house had been baptized, she invited us, "Come and stay in my house if you have decided that I am a true believer in the Lord." And she persuaded us to go.

In Prison at Philippi

[16] One day as we were going to the place of prayer, we were met by a young servant woman who had an evil spirit that enabled her

to predict the future. She earned a lot of money for her owners by telling fortunes. [17]She followed Paul and us, shouting, "These men are servants of the Most High God! They announce to you how you can be saved!" [18]She did this for many days, until Paul became so upset that he turned round and said to the spirit, "In the name of Jesus Christ I order you to come out of her!" The spirit went out of her that very moment.

[19]When her owners realized that their chance of making money was gone, they seized Paul and Silas and dragged them to the authorities in the public square. [20]They brought them before the Roman officials and said, "These men are Jews, and they are causing trouble in our city. [21]They are teaching customs that are against our law; we are Roman citizens, and we cannot accept these customs or practise them." [22]And the crowd joined in the attack against Paul and Silas.

Then the officials tore the clothes off Paul and Silas and ordered them to be whipped. [23]After a severe beating, they were thrown into jail, and the jailer was ordered to lock them up tight. [24]Upon receiving this order, the jailer threw them into the inner cell and fastened their feet between heavy blocks of wood.

[25]About midnight Paul and Silas were praying and singing hymns to God, and the other prisoners were listening to them. [26]Suddenly there was a violent earthquake, which shook the prison to its foundations. At once all the doors opened, and the chains fell off all the prisoners. [27]The jailer woke up, and when he saw the prison doors open, he thought that the prisoners had escaped; so he pulled out his sword and was about to kill himself. [28]But Paul shouted at the top of his voice, "Don't harm yourself! We are all here!"

[29]The jailer called for a light, rushed in, and fell trembling at the feet of Paul and Silas. [30]Then he led them out and asked, "Sirs, what must I do to be saved?"

[31]They answered, "Believe in the Lord Jesus, and you will be saved — you and your family." [32]Then they preached the word of the Lord to him and to all the others in his house. [33]At that very hour of the night the jailer took them and washed their wounds; and he and all his family were baptized at once. [34]Then he took Paul and Silas up into his house and gave them some food to eat. He and his family were filled with joy, because they now believed in God.

[35]The next morning the Roman authorities sent police officers with the order, "Let those men go."

36 So the jailer told Paul, "The officials have sent an order for you and Silas to be released. You may leave, then, and go in peace."

37 But Paul said to the police officers, "We were not found guilty of any crime, yet they whipped us in public — and we are Roman citizens! Then they threw us in prison. And now they want to send us away secretly. Not likely! The Roman officials themselves must come here and let us out."

38 The police officers reported these words to the Roman officials; and when they heard that Paul and Silas were Roman citizens, they were afraid. 39 So they went and apologized to them; then they led them out of the prison and asked them to leave the city. 40 Paul and Silas left the prison and went to Lydia's house. There they met the believers, spoke words of encouragement to them, and left.

In Thessalonica

[1] Paul and Silas travelled on through Amphipolis and Apollonia and came to Thessalonica, where there was a synagogue. [2] According to his usual habit Paul went to the synagogue. There during three Sabbaths he held discussions with the people, quoting [3] and explaining the Scriptures and proving from them that the Messiah had to suffer and rise from death. "This Jesus whom I announce to you," Paul said, "is the Messiah." [4] Some of them were convinced and joined Paul and Silas; so did many of the leading women and a large group of Greeks who worshipped God.

[5] But some Jews were jealous and gathered worthless loafers from the streets and formed a mob. They set the whole city in an uproar and attacked the home of a man called Jason, in an attempt to find Paul and Silas and bring them out to the people. [6] But when they did not find them, they dragged Jason and some other believers before the city authorities and shouted, "These men have caused trouble everywhere! Now they have come to our city, [7] and Jason has kept them in his house. They are all breaking the laws of the Emperor, saying that there is another king, whose name is Jesus." [8] With these words they threw the crowd and the city authorities into an uproar. [9] The authorities made Jason and the others pay the required amount of money to be released, and then let them go.

In Berea

[10] As soon as night came, the believers sent Paul and Silas to Berea. When they arrived, they went to the synagogue. [11] The people there were more open-minded than the people in Thessalonica. They listened to the message with great eagerness, and every day they studied the Scriptures to see if what Paul said was really true. [12] Many of them believed; and many Greek women of high social standing and many Greek men also believed. [13] But when the Jews in Thessalonica heard that Paul had preached the word of God in Berea also, they came there and started exciting and stirring up the mob. [14] At once the believers sent Paul away to the coast; but both Silas and Timothy stayed in Berea. [15] The men who were taking Paul went with him as far as Athens and then returned to Berea with instructions from Paul that Silas and Timothy should join him as soon as possible.

In Athens

[16] While Paul was waiting in Athens for Silas and Timothy, he was greatly upset when he noticed how full of idols the city was. [17] So he

held discussions in the synagogue with the Jews and with the Gentiles who worshipped God, and also in the public square every day with the people who happened to pass by. [18] Certain Epicurean and Stoic teachers also debated with him. Some of them asked, "What is this ignorant show-off trying to say?"

Others answered, "He seems to be talking about foreign gods." They said this because Paul was preaching about Jesus and the resurrection. [19] So they took Paul, brought him before the city council, the Areopagus, and said, "We would like to know what this new teaching is that you are talking about. [20] Some of the things we hear you say sound strange to us, and we would like to know what they mean." [21] (For all the citizens of Athens and the foreigners who lived there liked to spend all their time telling and hearing the latest new thing.)

[22] Paul stood up in front of the city council and said, "I see that in every way you Athenians are very religious. [23] For as I walked through your city and looked at the places where you worship, I found an altar on which is written, 'To an Unknown God'. That which you worship, then, even though you do not know it, is what I now proclaim to you. [24] God, who made the world and everything in it, is Lord of heaven and earth and does not live in temples made by human hands. [25] Nor does he need anything that we can supply by working for him, since it is he himself who gives life and breath and everything else to everyone. [26] From one human being he created all races on earth and made them live throughout the whole earth. He himself fixed beforehand the exact times and the limits of the places where they would live. [27] He did this so that they would look for him, and perhaps find him as they felt about for him. Yet God is actually not far from any one of us; [28] as someone has said,

'In him we live and move and exist.'

It is as some of your poets have said,

'We too are his children.'

[29] Since we are God's children, we should not suppose that his nature is anything like an image of gold or silver or stone, shaped by human art and skill. [30] God has overlooked the times when people did not know him, but now he commands all of them everywhere to turn away from their evil ways. [31] For he has fixed a day in which he will judge the whole world with justice by means of a man he has chosen. He has given proof of this to everyone by raising that man from death!"

[32] When they heard Paul speak about a raising from death, some of them made fun of him, but others said, "We want to hear you speak

about this again." [33] And so Paul left the meeting. [34] Some men joined him and believed, among whom was Dionysius, a member of the council; there was also a woman named Damaris, and some other people.

In Corinth

[1] After this, Paul left Athens and went on to Corinth. [2] There he met a Jew named Aquila, born in Pontus, who had recently come from Italy with his wife Priscilla, for the Emperor Claudius had ordered all the Jews to leave Rome. Paul went to see them, [3] and stayed and worked with them, because he earned his living by making tents, just as they did. [4] He held discussions in the synagogue every Sabbath, trying to convince both Jews and Greeks.

[5] When Silas and Timothy arrived from Macedonia, Paul gave his whole time to preaching the message, testifying to the Jews that Jesus is the Messiah. [6] When they opposed him and said evil things about him, he protested by shaking the dust from his clothes and saying to them, "If you are lost, you yourselves must take the blame for it! I am not responsible. From now on I will go to the Gentiles." [7] So he left them and went to live in the house of a Gentile named Titius Justus, who worshipped God; his house was next to the synagogue. [8] Crispus, who was the leader of the synagogue, believed in the Lord, together with all his family; and many other people in Corinth heard the message, believed, and were baptized.

[9] One night Paul had a vision in which the Lord said to him, "Do not be afraid, but keep on speaking and do not give up, [10] for I am with you. No one will be able to harm you, for many in this city are my people." [11] So Paul stayed there for a year and a half, teaching the people the word of God.

[12] When Gallio was made the Roman governor of Achaia, Jews there got together, seized Paul, and took him into court. [13] "This man," they said, "is trying to persuade people to worship God in a way that is against the law!"

[14] Paul was about to speak when Gallio said to the Jews, "If this were a matter of some evil crime or wrong that has been committed, it would be reasonable for me to be patient with you Jews. [15] But since it is an argument about words and names and your own law, you yourselves must settle it. I will not be the judge of such things!" [16] And he drove them out of the court. [17] They all seized Sosthenes, the leader of the synagogue, and beat him in front of the court. But that did not bother Gallio a bit.

The Return to Antioch

[18] Paul stayed on with the believers in Corinth for many days, then left them and sailed off with Priscilla and Aquila for Syria. Before sailing

from Cenchreae he had his head shaved because of a vow he had taken. [19] They arrived in Ephesus, where Paul left Priscilla and Aquila. He went into the synagogue and held discussions with the Jews. [20] The people asked him to stay longer, but he would not consent. [21] Instead, he told them as he left, "If it is the will of God, I will come back to you." And so he sailed from Ephesus.

[22] When he arrived at Caesarea, he went to Jerusalem and greeted the church, and then went to Antioch. [23] After spending some time there, he left and went through the region of Galatia and Phrygia, strengthening all the believers.

Apollos in Ephesus and Corinth

[24] At that time a Jew named Apollos, who had been born in Alexandria, came to Ephesus. He was an eloquent speaker and had a thorough knowledge of the Scriptures. [25] He had been instructed in the Way of the Lord, and with great enthusiasm he proclaimed and taught correctly the facts about Jesus. However, he knew only the baptism of John. [26] He began to speak boldly in the synagogue. When Priscilla and Aquila heard him, they took him home with them and explained to him more correctly the Way of God. [27] Apollos then decided to go to Achaia, so the believers in Ephesus helped him by writing to the believers in Achaia, urging them to welcome him. When he arrived, he was a great help to those who through God's grace had become believers. [28] For with his strong arguments he defeated the Jews in public debates by proving from the Scriptures that Jesus is the Messiah.

Paul in Ephesus

[1] While Apollos was in Corinth, Paul travelled through the interior of the province and arrived in Ephesus. There he found some disciples [2] and asked them, "Did you receive the Holy Spirit when you became believers?"

"We have not even heard that there is a Holy Spirit," they answered.

[3] "Well, then, what kind of baptism did you receive?" Paul asked.

"The baptism of John," they answered.

[4] Paul said, "The baptism of John was for those who turned from their sins; and he told the people of Israel to believe in the one who was coming after him — that is, in Jesus."

[5] When they heard this, they were baptized in the name of the Lord Jesus. [6] Paul placed his hands on them, and the Holy Spirit came upon them; they spoke in strange tongues and also proclaimed God's message. [7] They were about twelve men in all.

[8] Paul went into the synagogue and during three months spoke boldly with the people, holding discussions with them and trying to convince them about the Kingdom of God. [9] But some of them were stubborn and would not believe, and before the whole group they said evil things about the Way of the Lord. So Paul left them and took the believers with him, and every day he held discussions in the lecture hall of Tyrannus. [10] This went on for two years, so that all the people who lived in the province of Asia, both Jews and Gentiles, heard the word of the Lord.

The Sons of Sceva

[11] God was performing unusual miracles through Paul. [12] Even handkerchiefs and aprons he had used were taken to those who were ill, and their diseases were driven away, and the evil spirits would go out of them. [13] Some Jews who travelled round and drove out evil spirits also tried to use the name of the Lord Jesus to do this. They said to the evil spirits, "I command you in the name of Jesus, whom Paul preaches." [14] Seven brothers, who were the sons of a Jewish High Priest named Sceva, were doing this.

[15] But the evil spirit said to them, "I know Jesus, and I know about Paul; but you — who are you?"

[16] The man who had the evil spirit in him attacked them with such violence that he overpowered them all. They ran away from his house,

wounded and with their clothes torn off. [17] All the Jews and Gentiles who lived in Ephesus heard about this; they were all filled with fear, and the name of the Lord Jesus was given greater honour. [18] Many of the believers came, publicly admitting and revealing what they had done. [19] Many of those who had practised magic brought their books together and burnt them in public. They added up the price of the books, and the total came to 50,000 silver coins. [20] In this powerful way the word of the Lord kept spreading and growing stronger.

The Riot in Ephesus

[21] After these things had happened, Paul made up his mind to travel through Macedonia and Achaia and go on to Jerusalem. "After I go there," he said, "I must also see Rome." [22] So he sent Timothy and Erastus, two of his helpers, to Macedonia, while he spent more time in the province of Asia.

[23] It was at this time that there was serious trouble in Ephesus because of the Way of the Lord. [24] A certain silversmith named Demetrius made silver models of the temple of the goddess Artemis, and his business brought a great deal of profit to the workers. [25] So he called them all together with others whose work was like theirs and said to them, "Men, you know that our prosperity comes from this work. [26] Now, you can see and hear for yourselves what this fellow Paul is doing. He says that gods made by human hands are not gods at all, and he has succeeded in convincing many people, both here in Ephesus and in nearly the whole province of Asia. [27] There is the danger, then, that this business of ours will get a bad name. Not only that, but there is also the danger that the temple of the great goddess Artemis will come to mean nothing and that her greatness will be destroyed — the goddess worshipped by everyone in Asia and in all the world!"

[28] As the crowd heard these words, they became furious and started shouting, "Great is Artemis of Ephesus!" [29] The uproar spread throughout the whole city. The mob seized Gaius and Aristarchus, two Macedonians who were travelling with Paul, and rushed with them to the theatre. [30] Paul himself wanted to go before the crowd, but the believers would not let him. [31] Some of the provincial authorities, who were his friends, also sent him a message begging him not to show himself in the theatre. [32] Meanwhile the whole meeting was in an uproar: some people were shouting one thing, others were shouting something else, because most of them did not even know why they had come together. [33] Some of the people concluded that Alexander

was responsible, since the Jews made him go up to the front. Then Alexander motioned with his hand for the people to be silent, and he tried to make a speech of defence. [34] But when they recognized that he was a Jew, they all shouted together the same thing for two hours: "Great is Artemis of Ephesus!"

[35] At last the town clerk was able to calm the crowd. "Fellow-Ephesians!" he said. "Everyone knows that the city of Ephesus is the keeper of the temple of the great Artemis and of the sacred stone that fell down from heaven. [36] Nobody can deny these things. So then, you must calm down and not do anything reckless. [37] You have brought these men here even though they have not robbed temples or said evil things about our goddess. [38] If Demetrius and his workers have an accusation against anyone, we have the authorities and the regular days for court; charges can be made there. [39] But if there is something more that you want, it will have to be settled in a legal meeting of citizens. [40] For after what has happened today, there is the danger that we will be accused of a riot. There is no excuse for all this uproar, and we would not be able to give a good reason for it." [41] After saying this, he dismissed the meeting.

To Macedonia and Achaia

[1] After the uproar died down, Paul called together the believers and with words of encouragement said goodbye to them. Then he left and went on to Macedonia. [2] He went through those regions and encouraged the people with many messages. Then he came to Achaia, [3] where he stayed three months. He was getting ready to go to Syria when he discovered that there were Jews plotting against him; so he decided to go back through Macedonia. [4] Sopater son of Pyrrhus, from Berea, went with him; so did Aristarchus and Secundus, from Thessalonica; Gaius, from Derbe; Tychicus and Trophimus, from the province of Asia; and Timothy. [5] They went ahead and waited for us in Troas. [6] We sailed from Philippi after the Festival of Unleavened Bread, and five days later we joined them in Troas, where we spent a week.

Paul's Last Visit to Troas

[7] On Saturday evening we gathered together for the fellowship meal. Paul spoke to the people and kept on speaking until midnight, since he was going to leave the next day. [8] Many lamps were burning in the upstairs room where we were meeting. [9] A young man named Eutychus was sitting in the window, and as Paul kept on talking, Eutychus got sleepier and sleepier, until he finally went sound asleep and fell from the third storey to the ground. When they picked him up, he was dead. [10] But Paul went down and threw himself on him and hugged him. "Don't worry," he said, "he is still alive!" [11] Then he went back upstairs, broke bread, and ate. After talking with them for a long time, even until sunrise, Paul left. [12] They took the young man home alive and were greatly comforted.

From Troas to Miletus

[13] We went on ahead to the ship and sailed off to Assos, where we were going to take Paul aboard. He had told us to do this, because he was going there by land. [14] When he met us in Assos, we took him aboard and went on to Mitylene. [15] We sailed from there and arrived off Chios the next day. A day later we came to Samos, and the following day we reached Miletus. [16] Paul had decided to sail on past Ephesus, so as not to lose any time in the province of Asia. He was in a hurry to arrive in Jerusalem by the day of Pentecost, if at all possible.

Paul's Farewell Speech to the Elders of Ephesus

[17] From Miletus Paul sent a message to Ephesus, asking the elders of the church to meet him. [18] When they arrived, he said to them, "You

know how I spent the whole time I was with you, from the first day I arrived in the province of Asia. [19] With all humility and many tears I did my work as the Lord's servant during the hard times that came to me because of the plots of some Jews. [20] You know that I did not hold back anything that would be of help to you as I preached and taught in public and in your homes. [21] To Jews and Gentiles alike I gave solemn warning that they should turn from their sins to God and believe in our Lord Jesus. [22] And now, in obedience to the Holy Spirit I am going to Jerusalem, not knowing what will happen to me there. [23] I only know that in every city the Holy Spirit has warned me that prison and troubles wait for me. [24] But I reckon my own life to be worth nothing to me; I only want to complete my mission and finish the work that the Lord Jesus gave me to do, which is to declare the Good News about the grace of God.

[25] "I have gone about among all of you, preaching the Kingdom of God. And now I know that none of you will ever see me again. [26] So I solemnly declare to you this very day: if any of you should be lost, I am not responsible. [27] For I have not held back from announcing to you the whole purpose of God. [28] So keep watch over yourselves and over all the flock which the Holy Spirit has placed in your care. Be shepherds of the church of God, which he made his own through the blood of his Son. [29] I know that after I leave, fierce wolves will come among you, and they will not spare the flock. [30] The time will come when some men from your own group will tell lies to lead the believers away after them. [31] Watch, then, and remember that with many tears, day and night, I taught every one of you for three years.

[32] "And now I commend you to the care of God and to the message of his grace, which is able to build you up and give you the blessings God has for all his people. [33] I have not wanted anyone's silver or gold or clothing. [34] You yourselves know that I have worked with these hands of mine to provide everything that my companions and I have needed. [35] I have shown you in all things that by working hard in this way we must help the weak, remembering the words that the Lord Jesus himself said, 'There is more happiness in giving than in receiving.'"

[36] When Paul finished, he knelt down with them and prayed. [37] They were all crying as they hugged him and kissed him goodbye. [38] They were especially sad because he had said that they would never see him again. And so they went with him to the ship.

"But I reckon my own life to be worth nothing to me; I only want to complete my mission and finish the work that the Lord Jesus gave me to do, which is to declare the Good News about the grace of God."

Acts 20.24

Reflect

Paul is clear that his travel plans have been shaped by the Holy Spirit. Through the Spirit he has fully embraced God, and through that he knows who he really is, and what God wants him to do. It is this which leads him to talk about his 'mission' or 'being sent'.

Being sent by the Holy Spirit doesn't mean that Paul won't face any difficulties – far from it. But his experience of Jesus, through the power of the Holy Spirit and the grace of God, gives him the courage to overcome any fears and troubles which lie ahead of him.

We're all called to mission, but it's going to be different for everyone. Paul's audience is the people of Jerusalem, and then later the people of Rome – the two major cities in his world. But we're sent out amongst different people – our families, our communities, where we work, even those we may be in hospital or prison with. Those are the people God is sending us to – to show them love, kindness and caring, and the grace of God, a gift we're given and a gift we're called to pass on.

Do you remember a time when you were sent on a mission by somebody? How did it feel? How do you think God's mission for you might feel different, and what kind of mission do you think God might be sending you on?

Pray

Lord God, the commander of my mission,
guide me and protect me through the Holy Spirit.
Through you I know who I am,
and I am ready to be sent out by you.
Open my eyes to my mission,
and, wherever I am sent,
help me to bring love where there is hate,
and light where there is darkness.
Amen

Act

Is there a verse or passage in this book, or anywhere else in
the Bible, which inspires you in your mission? It could also be a
prayer you've heard, or even a quote from someone famous.
If you can't think of anything, try talking to a priest, pastor or
chaplain. Whatever it is, write it down and put it somewhere
you'll see regularly – maybe by the mirror, fridge, or even inside
your favourite book, so you are reminded daily of being sent.

Paul Goes to Jerusalem

¹We said goodbye to them and left. After sailing straight across, we came to Cos; the next day we reached Rhodes, and from there we went on to Patara. ²There we found a ship that was going to Phoenicia, so we went aboard and sailed away. ³We came to where we could see Cyprus, and then sailed south of it on to Syria. We went ashore at Tyre, where the ship was going to unload its cargo. ⁴There we found some believers and stayed with them a week. By the power of the Spirit they told Paul not to go to Jerusalem. ⁵But when our time with them was over, we left and went on our way. All of them, together with their wives and children, went with us out of the city to the beach, where we all knelt and prayed. ⁶Then we said goodbye to one another, and we went on board the ship while they went back home.

⁷We continued our voyage, sailing from Tyre to Ptolemais, where we greeted the believers and stayed with them for a day. ⁸On the following day we left and arrived in Caesarea. There we stayed at the house of Philip the evangelist, one of the seven men who had been chosen as helpers in Jerusalem. ⁹He had four unmarried daughters who proclaimed God's message. ¹⁰We had been there for several days when a prophet named Agabus arrived from Judea. ¹¹He came to us, took Paul's belt, tied up his own feet and hands with it, and said, "This is what the Holy Spirit says: The owner of this belt will be tied up in this way by the Jews in Jerusalem, and they will hand him over to the Gentiles."

¹²When we heard this, we and the others there begged Paul not to go to Jerusalem. ¹³But he answered, "What are you doing, crying like this and breaking my heart? I am ready not only to be tied up in Jerusalem but even to die there for the sake of the Lord Jesus."

¹⁴We could not convince him, so we gave up and said, "May the Lord's will be done."

¹⁵After spending some time there, we got our things ready and left for Jerusalem. ¹⁶Some of the disciples from Caesarea also went with us and took us to the house of the man we were going to stay with — Mnason, from Cyprus, who had been a believer since the early days.

Paul Visits James

¹⁷When we arrived in Jerusalem, the believers welcomed us warmly. ¹⁸The next day Paul went with us to see James; and all the church elders were present. ¹⁹Paul greeted them and gave a complete report

of everything that God had done among the Gentiles through his work. [20] After hearing him, they all praised God. Then they said, "Brother Paul, you can see how many thousands of Jews have become believers, and how devoted they all are to the Law. [21] They have been told that you have been teaching all the Jews who live in Gentile countries to abandon the Law of Moses, telling them not to circumcise their children or follow the Jewish customs. [22] They are sure to hear that you have arrived. What should be done, then? [23] This is what we want you to do. There are four men here who have taken a vow. [24] Go along with them and join them in the ceremony of purification and pay their expenses; then they will be able to shave their heads. In this way everyone will know that there is no truth in any of the things that they have been told about you, but that you yourself live in accordance with the Law of Moses. [25] But as for the Gentiles who have become believers, we have sent them a letter telling them we decided that they must not eat any food that has been offered to idols, or any blood, or any animal that has been strangled, and that they must keep themselves from sexual immorality."

[26] So Paul took the men and the next day performed the ceremony of purification with them. Then he went into the Temple and gave notice of how many days it would be until the end of the period of purification, when a sacrifice would be offered for each one of them.

Paul is Arrested in the Temple

[27] But just when the seven days were about to come to an end, some Jews from the province of Asia saw Paul in the Temple. They stirred up the whole crowd and seized Paul. [28] "Men of Israel!" they shouted. "Help! This is the man who goes everywhere teaching everyone against the people of Israel, the Law of Moses, and this Temple. And now he has even brought some Gentiles into the Temple and defiled this holy place!" [29] (They said this because they had seen Trophimus from Ephesus with Paul in the city, and they thought that Paul had taken him into the Temple.)

[30] Confusion spread through the whole city, and the people all ran together, seized Paul, and dragged him out of the Temple. At once the Temple doors were closed. [31] The mob was trying to kill Paul, when a report was sent up to the commander of the Roman troops that all Jerusalem was rioting. [32] At once the commander took some officers and soldiers and rushed down to the crowd. When the people saw him with the soldiers, they stopped beating Paul. [33] The commander

went over to Paul, arrested him, and ordered him to be bound with two chains. Then he asked, "Who is this man, and what has he done?" [34] Some in the crowd shouted one thing, others something else. There was such confusion that the commander could not find out exactly what had happened, so he ordered his men to take Paul up into the fort. [35] They got as far as the steps with him, and then the soldiers had to carry him because the mob was so wild. [36] They were all coming after him and screaming, "Kill him!"

Paul Defends Himself

[37] As the soldiers were about to take Paul into the fort, he spoke to the commander: "May I say something to you?"

"You speak Greek, do you?" the commander asked. [38] "Then you are not that Egyptian fellow who some time ago started a revolution and led 4,000 armed terrorists out into the desert?"

[39] Paul answered, "I am a Jew, born in Tarsus in Cilicia, a citizen of an important city. Please let me speak to the people."

[40] The commander gave him permission, so Paul stood on the steps and motioned with his hand for the people to be silent. When they were quiet, Paul spoke to them in Hebrew:

[1] "My fellow-Jews, listen to me as I make my defence before you!" [2] When they heard him speaking to them in Hebrew, they became even quieter; and Paul went on:

[3] "I am a Jew, born in Tarsus in Cilicia, but brought up here in Jerusalem as a student of Gamaliel. I received strict instruction in the Law of our ancestors and was just as dedicated to God as are all of you who are here today. [4] I persecuted to the death the people who followed this Way. I arrested men and women and threw them into prison. [5] The High Priest and the whole Council can prove that I am telling the truth. I received from them letters written to fellow-Jews in Damascus, so I went there to arrest these people and bring them back in chains to Jerusalem to be punished.

Paul Tells of his Conversion

[6] "As I was travelling and coming near Damascus, about midday a bright light from the sky flashed suddenly round me. [7] I fell to the ground and heard a voice saying to me, 'Saul, Saul! Why do you persecute me?' [8] 'Who are you, Lord?' I asked. 'I am Jesus of Nazareth, whom you persecute,' he said to me. [9] The men with me saw the light, but did not hear the voice of the one who was speaking to me. [10] I asked, 'What shall I do, Lord?' and the Lord said to me, 'Get up and go into Damascus, and there you will be told everything that God has determined for you to do.' [11] I was blind because of the bright light, and so my companions took me by the hand and led me into Damascus.

[12] "In that city was a man named Ananias, a religious man who obeyed our Law and was highly respected by all the Jews living there. [13] He came to me, stood by me, and said, 'Brother Saul, see again!' At that very moment I saw again and looked at him. [14] He said, 'The God of our ancestors has chosen you to know his will, to see his righteous Servant, and to hear him speaking with his own voice. [15] For you will be a witness for him to tell everyone what you have seen and heard. [16] And now, why wait any longer? Get up and be baptized and have your sins washed away by praying to him.'

Paul's Call to Preach to the Gentiles

[17] "I went back to Jerusalem, and while I was praying in the Temple, I had a vision, [18] in which I saw the Lord, as he said to me, 'Hurry and leave Jerusalem quickly, because the people here will not accept your witness about me.' [19] 'Lord,' I answered, 'they know very well that

I went to the synagogues and arrested and beat those who believe in you. [20] And when your witness Stephen was put to death, I myself was there, approving of his murder and taking care of the cloaks of his murderers.' [21] 'Go,' the Lord said to me, 'for I will send you far away to the Gentiles.'"

[22] The people listened to Paul until he said this; but then they started shouting at the top of their voices, "Away with him! Kill him! He's not fit to live!" [23] They were screaming, waving their clothes, and throwing dust up in the air. [24] The Roman commander ordered his men to take Paul into the fort, and he told them to whip him in order to find out why the Jews were screaming like this against him. [25] But when they had tied him up to be whipped, Paul said to the officer standing there, "Is it lawful for you to whip a Roman citizen who hasn't even been tried for any crime?"

[26] When the officer heard this, he went to the commander and asked him, "What are you doing? That man is a Roman citizen!"

[27] So the commander went to Paul and asked him, "Tell me, are you a Roman citizen?"

"Yes," answered Paul.

[28] The commander said, "I became one by paying a large amount of money."

"But I am one by birth," Paul answered.

[29] At once the men who were going to question Paul drew back from him; and the commander was frightened when he realized that Paul was a Roman citizen and that he had put him in chains.

Paul before the Council

[30] The commander wanted to find out for certain what the Jews were accusing Paul of; so the next day he had Paul's chains taken off and ordered the chief priests and the whole Council to meet. Then he took Paul and made him stand before them.

¹ Paul looked straight at the Council and said, "My fellow-Israelites! My conscience is perfectly clear about the way in which I have lived before God to this very day." ² The High Priest Ananias ordered those who were standing close to Paul to strike him on the mouth. ³ Paul said to him, "God will certainly strike you — you whitewashed wall! You sit there to judge me according to the Law, yet you break the Law by ordering them to strike me!"

⁴ The men close to Paul said to him, "You are insulting God's High Priest!"

⁵ Paul answered, "My fellow-Israelites, I did not know that he was the High Priest. The scripture says, 'You must not speak evil of the ruler of your people.'"

⁶ When Paul saw that some of the group were Sadducees and the others were Pharisees, he called out in the Council, "Fellow-Israelites! I am a Pharisee, the son of Pharisees. I am on trial here because of the hope I have that the dead will rise to life!"

⁷ As soon as he said this, the Pharisees and Sadducees started to quarrel, and the group was divided. ⁸ (For the Sadducees say that people will not rise from death and that there are no angels or spirits; but the Pharisees believe in all three.) ⁹ The shouting became louder, and some of the teachers of the Law who belonged to the party of the Pharisees stood up and protested strongly: "We cannot find anything wrong with this man! Perhaps a spirit or an angel really did speak to him!"

¹⁰ The argument became so violent that the commander was afraid that Paul would be torn to pieces. So he ordered his soldiers to go down into the group, get Paul away from them, and take him into the fort.

¹¹ That night the Lord stood by Paul and said, "Don't be afraid! You have given your witness for me here in Jerusalem, and you must also do the same in Rome."

The Plot against Paul's Life

¹² The next morning some Jews met together and made a plan. They took a vow that they would not eat or drink anything until they had killed Paul. ¹³ There were more than forty who planned this together. ¹⁴ Then they went to the chief priests and elders and said, "We have taken a solemn vow together not to eat a thing until we have killed Paul. ¹⁵ Now then, you and the Council send word to the Roman

commander to bring Paul down to you, pretending that you want to get more accurate information about him. But we will be ready to kill him before he ever gets here."

[16] But the son of Paul's sister heard about the plot; so he went to the fort and told Paul. [17] Then Paul called one of the officers and said to him, "Take this young man to the commander; he has something to tell him." [18] The officer took him, led him to the commander, and said, "The prisoner Paul called me and asked me to bring this young man to you, because he has something to say to you."

[19] The commander took him by the hand, led him off by himself, and asked him, "What have you got to tell me?"

[20] He said, "The Jewish authorities have agreed to ask you tomorrow to take Paul down to the Council, pretending that the Council wants to get more accurate information about him. [21] But don't listen to them, because there are more than forty men who will be hiding and waiting for him. They have taken a vow not to eat or drink until they have killed him. They are now ready to do it and are waiting for your decision."

[22] The commander said, "Don't tell anyone that you have reported this to me." And he sent the young man away.

Paul is Sent to Governor Felix

[23] Then the commander called two of his officers and said, "Get 200 soldiers ready to go to Caesarea, together with seventy horsemen and 200 spearmen, and be ready to leave by nine o'clock tonight. [24] Provide some horses for Paul to ride and get him safely through to the governor Felix." [25] Then the commander wrote a letter that went like this:

[26] "Claudius Lysias to His Excellency, the governor Felix: Greetings. [27] The Jews seized this man and were about to kill him. I learnt that he was a Roman citizen, so I went with my soldiers and rescued him. [28] I wanted to know what they were accusing him of, so I took him down to their Council. [29] I found out that he had not done anything for which he deserved to die or be put in prison; the accusation against him had to do with questions about their own law. [30] And when I was informed that there was a plot against him, at once I decided to send him to you. I have told his accusers to make their charges against him before you."

[31] The soldiers carried out their orders. They got Paul and took him that night as far as Antipatris. [32] The next day the foot soldiers returned to

the fort and left the horsemen to go on with him. [33] They took him to Caesarea, delivered the letter to the governor, and handed Paul over to him. [34] The governor read the letter and asked Paul what province he was from. When he found out that he was from Cilicia, [35] he said, "I will hear you when your accusers arrive." Then he gave orders for Paul to be kept under guard in the governor's headquarters.

The Case Against Paul

[1] Five days later the High Priest Ananias went to Caesarea with some elders and a lawyer named Tertullus. They appeared before Felix and made their charges against Paul. [2] Then Paul was called in, and Tertullus began to make his accusation, as follows:

"Your Excellency! Your wise leadership has brought us a long period of peace, and many necessary reforms are being made for the good of our country. [3] We welcome this everywhere and at all times, and we are deeply grateful to you. [4] I do not want to take up too much of your time, however, so I beg you to be kind and listen to our brief account. [5] We found this man to be a dangerous nuisance; he starts riots among Jews all over the world and is a leader of the party of the Nazarenes. [6] He also tried to defile the Temple, and we arrested him. [8] If you question this man, you yourself will be able to learn from him all the things that we are accusing him of." [9] The Jews joined in the accusation and said that all this was true.

Paul's Defence before Felix

[10] The governor then motioned to Paul to speak, and Paul said,

"I know that you have been a judge over this nation for many years, and so I am happy to defend myself before you. [11] As you can find out for yourself, it was no more than twelve days ago that I went to Jerusalem to worship. [12] The Jews did not find me arguing with anyone in the Temple, nor did they find me stirring up the people, either in the synagogues or anywhere else in the city. [13] Nor can they give you proof of the accusations they now bring against me. [14] I do admit this to you: I worship the God of our ancestors by following that Way which they say is false. But I also believe in everything written in the Law of Moses and the books of the prophets. [15] I have the same hope in God that these themselves have, namely, that all people, both the good and the bad, will rise from death. [16] And so I do my best always to have a clear conscience before God and human beings.

[17] "After being away from Jerusalem for several years, I went there to take some money to my own people and to offer sacrifices. [18] It was while I was doing this that they found me in the Temple after I had completed the ceremony of purification. There was no crowd with me and no disorder. [19] But some Jews from the province of Asia were there; they themselves ought to come before you and make their accusations if they have anything against me. [20] Or let these who are here tell what crime they found me guilty of when I stood before the Council — [21] except for

the one thing I called out when I stood before them: 'I am being tried by you today for believing that the dead will rise to life.'"

[22] Then Felix, who was well informed about the Way, brought the hearing to a close. "When Lysias the commander arrives," he told them, "I will decide your case." [23] He ordered the officer in charge of Paul to keep him under guard, but to give him some freedom and allow his friends to provide for his needs.

Paul before Felix and Drusilla

[24] After some days Felix came with his wife Drusilla, who was Jewish. He sent for Paul and listened to him as he talked about faith in Christ Jesus. [25] But as Paul went on discussing about goodness, self-control, and the coming Day of Judgement, Felix was afraid and said, "You may leave now. I will call you again when I get the chance." [26] At the same time he was hoping that Paul would give him some money; and for this reason he would often send for him and talk with him.

[27] After two years had passed, Porcius Festus succeeded Felix as governor. Felix wanted to gain favour with the Jews so he left Paul in prison.

Paul Appeals to the Emperor

[1] Three days after Festus arrived in the province, he went from Caesarea to Jerusalem, [2] where the chief priests and the Jewish leaders brought their charges against Paul. They begged Festus [3] to do them the favour of bringing Paul to Jerusalem, for they had made a plot to kill him on the way. [4] Festus answered, "Paul is being kept a prisoner in Caesarea, and I myself will be going back there soon. [5] Let your leaders go to Caesarea with me and accuse the man if he has done anything wrong."

[6] Festus spent another eight or ten days with them and then went to Caesarea. On the next day he sat down in the court of judgement and ordered Paul to be brought in. [7] When Paul arrived, the Jews who had come from Jerusalem stood round him and started making many serious charges against him, which they were not able to prove. [8] But Paul defended himself: "I have done nothing wrong against the Law of the Jews or against the Temple or against the Roman Emperor."

[9] But Festus wanted to gain favour with the Jews, so he asked Paul, "Would you be willing to go to Jerusalem and be tried on these charges before me there?"

[10] Paul said, "I am standing before the Emperor's own court of judgement, where I should be tried. I have done no wrong to the Jews, as you yourself well know. [11] If I have broken the law and done something for which I deserve the death penalty, I do not ask to escape it. But if there is no truth in the charges they bring against me, no one can hand me over to them. I appeal to the Emperor."

[12] Then Festus, after conferring with his advisers, answered, "You have appealed to the Emperor, so to the Emperor you will go."

Paul before Agrippa and Bernice

[13] Some time later King Agrippa and Bernice came to Caesarea to pay a visit of welcome to Festus. [14] After they had been there several days, Festus explained Paul's situation to the king: "There is a man here who was left a prisoner by Felix; [15] and when I went to Jerusalem, the Jewish chief priests and elders brought charges against him and asked me to condemn him. [16] But I told them that we Romans are not in the habit of handing over anyone accused of a crime before he has met his accusers face to face and has had the chance of defending himself against the accusation. [17] When they came here, then, I lost no time, but on the very next day I sat in the court and ordered the man to be

brought in. [18] His opponents stood up, but they did not accuse him of any of the evil crimes that I thought they would. [19] All they had were some arguments with him about their own religion and about a man named Jesus, who has died; but Paul claims that he is alive. [20] I was undecided about how I could get information on these matters, so I asked Paul if he would be willing to go to Jerusalem and be tried there on these charges. [21] But Paul appealed; he asked to be kept under guard and to let the Emperor decide his case. So I gave orders for him to be kept under guard until I could send him to the Emperor."

[22] Agrippa said to Festus, "I would like to hear this man myself."

"You will hear him tomorrow," Festus answered.

[23] The next day Agrippa and Bernice came with great pomp and ceremony and entered the audience hall with the military chiefs and the leading men of the city. Festus gave the order, and Paul was brought in. [24] Festus said, "King Agrippa and all who are here with us: You see this man against whom all the Jewish people, both here and in Jerusalem, have brought complaints to me. They scream that he should not live any longer. [25] But I could not find that he had done anything for which he deserved the death sentence. And since he himself made an appeal to the Emperor, I have decided to send him. [26] But I have nothing definite about him to write to the Emperor. So I have brought him here before you — and especially before you, King Agrippa! — so that, after investigating his case, I may have something to write. [27] For it seems unreasonable to me to send a prisoner without clearly indicating the charges against him."

Paul Defends Himself before Agrippa

[1] Agrippa said to Paul, "You have permission to speak on your own behalf." Paul stretched out his hand and defended himself as follows:

[2] "King Agrippa! I consider myself fortunate that today I am to defend myself before you from all the things these Jews accuse me of, [3] particularly since you know so well all the Jewish customs and disputes. I ask you, then, to listen to me with patience.

[4] "All the Jews know how I have lived ever since I was young. They know how I have spent my whole life, at first in my own country and then in Jerusalem. [5] They have always known, if they are willing to testify, that from the very first I have lived as a member of the strictest party of our religion, the Pharisees. [6] And now I stand here to be tried because of the hope I have in the promise that God made to our ancestors — [7] the very thing that the twelve tribes of our people hope to receive, as they worship God day and night. And it is because of this hope, Your Majesty, that I am being accused by these Jews! [8] Why do you who are here find it impossible to believe that God raises the dead?

[9] "I myself thought that I should do everything I could against the cause of Jesus of Nazareth. [10] That is what I did in Jerusalem. I received authority from the chief priests and put many of God's people in prison; and when they were sentenced to death, I also voted against them. [11] Many times I had them punished in the synagogues and tried to make them deny their faith. I was so furious with them that I even went to foreign cities to persecute them.

Paul Tells of his Conversion

[12] "It was for this purpose that I went to Damascus with authority and orders from the chief priests. [13] It was on the road at midday, Your Majesty, that I saw a light much brighter than the sun, coming from the sky and shining round me and the men travelling with me. [14] All of us fell to the ground, and I heard a voice say to me in Hebrew, 'Saul, Saul! Why are you persecuting me? You are hurting yourself by hitting back, like an ox kicking against its owner's stick.' [15] 'Who are you, Lord?' I asked. And the Lord answered, 'I am Jesus, whom you persecute. [16] But get up and stand on your feet. I have appeared to you to appoint you as my servant. You are to tell others what you have seen of me today and what I will show you in the future. [17] I will rescue you from the people of Israel and from the Gentiles to whom I will send you. [18] You are to open their eyes and turn them from the

darkness to the light and from the power of Satan to God, so that through their faith in me they will have their sins forgiven and receive their place among God's chosen people.'

Paul Tells of his Work

[19] "And so, King Agrippa, I did not disobey the vision I had from heaven. [20] First in Damascus and in Jerusalem and then in all Judea and among the Gentiles, I preached that they must repent of their sins and turn to God and do the things that would show they had repented. [21] It was for this reason that these Jews seized me while I was in the Temple, and they tried to kill me. [22] But to this very day I have been helped by God, and so I stand here giving my witness to all, to small and great alike. What I say is the very same thing which the prophets and Moses said was going to happen: [23] that the Messiah must suffer and be the first one to rise from death, to announce the light of salvation to the Jews and to the Gentiles."

[24] As Paul defended himself in this way, Festus shouted at him, "You are mad, Paul! Your great learning is driving you mad!"

[25] Paul answered, "I am not mad, Your Excellency! I am speaking the sober truth. [26] King Agrippa! I can speak to you with all boldness, because you know about these things. I am sure that you have taken notice of every one of them, for this thing has not happened hidden away in a corner. [27] King Agrippa, do you believe the prophets? I know that you do!"

[28] Agrippa said to Paul, "In this short time do you think you will make me a Christian?"

[29] "Whether a short time or a long time," Paul answered, "my prayer to God is that you and all the rest of you who are listening to me today might become what I am — except, of course, for these chains!"

[30] Then the king, the governor, Bernice, and all the others got up, [31] and after leaving they said to each other, "This man has not done anything for which he should die or be put in prison." [32] And Agrippa said to Festus, "This man could have been released if he had not appealed to the Emperor."

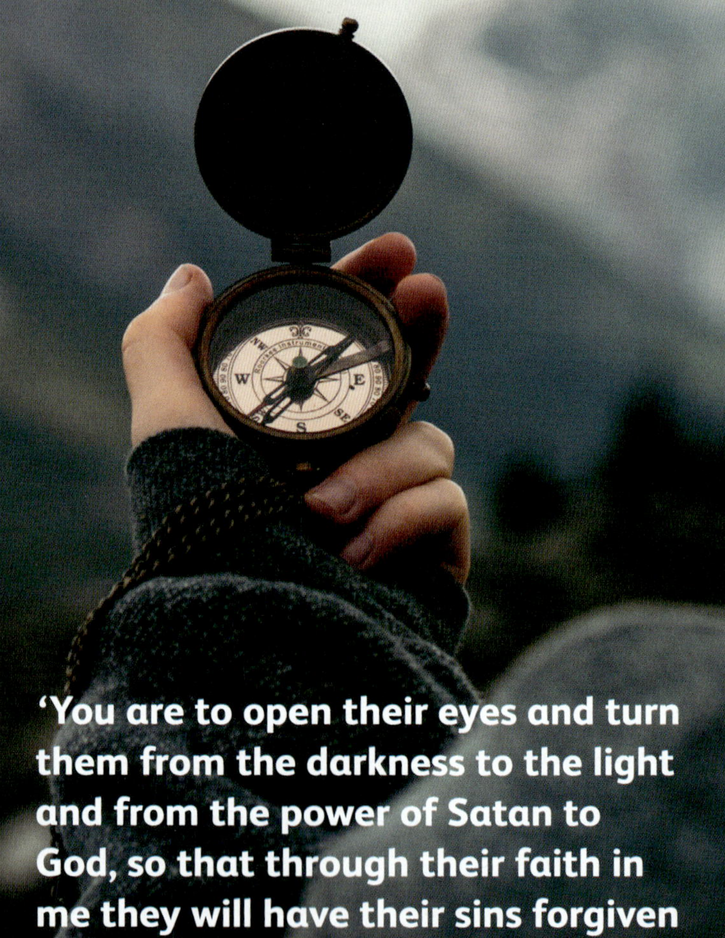
'You are to open their eyes and turn them from the darkness to the light and from the power of Satan to God, so that through their faith in me they will have their sins forgiven and receive their place among God's chosen people.'

Acts 26.18

Reflect

As Paul approaches his final journey, which will take him all the way to Rome, he retells the story of his encounter with Jesus on the road to Damascus back in Acts chapter 9 (page 120). It is his personal testimony, the story of how he came to follow Jesus. And Paul's experiences, his journey, and his mission, are rooted in his story, in who he is. Paul actively arrested followers of Jesus and tried to shut down Christianity before it could spread. Then, after encountering Jesus, he turned his life around, and went from trying to destroy the Church to helping it grow like never before.

But Paul is keen to tell his story as an ongoing story. The people he is sent to are to continue to find their place in the family of God, fulfilling the invitation of God to all of us. The plan continues, despite Paul's impending death in Rome. This is Paul's destiny – not just his meeting with Jesus, not his death in Rome, but turning from destroying the Church to helping it spread across the world and long into the future, all the way to you reading this right now.

Our destinies, our paths, may not be as striking as a blinding light from heaven. Sometimes, rather than being knocked to the ground, we simply stumble upon our path, our destiny, and the fulfilment of God's plan in our life. But they are rooted in our story, in who we are. We may, like Paul, even have to turn our lives completely around – from causing harm to bringing love and peace – but there is no shame in that, because there is no shame in who we are, and what God calls us to do.

Throughout this book you've been on a journey too, from Jesus' birth through to the birth of the Church. But at the same time, you've explored what this means for you – from the beginning of your faith, to exploring the path you're called to walk. If you root that in your story, and how you came to be the person you are today, can you see the beginning of God's plans in your own life? Where do you think they may lead?

Pray

Everlasting God,
our stories are connected to your great story.
Help me to see how my story shapes who I am today,
and who I will be tomorrow.
Through you I am challenged,
renewed,
empowered,
and sent on my journey.
Guide me onto the right path,
and lead me into my unique place in your kingdom.
Amen

Act

As you grow in your relationship with God, it can be really
useful to make a note or keep a diary of your thoughts, feelings
and insights. It will help you to see, in the long run, how God's
plans have unfolded in the story of your life. It can be a normal
diary, or more creative such as art or imagery. Consider starting
one today.

Paul Sails for Rome

¹When it was decided that we should sail to Italy, they handed Paul and some other prisoners over to Julius, an officer in the Roman regiment called "The Emperor's Regiment". ²We went aboard a ship from Adramyttium, which was ready to leave for the seaports of the province of Asia, and we sailed away. Aristarchus, a Macedonian from Thessalonica, was with us. ³The next day we arrived at Sidon. Julius was kind to Paul and allowed him to go and see his friends, to be given what he needed. ⁴We went on from there, and because the winds were blowing against us, we sailed on the sheltered side of the island of Cyprus. ⁵We crossed over the sea off Cilicia and Pamphylia and came to Myra in Lycia. ⁶There the officer found a ship from Alexandria that was going to sail for Italy, so he put us aboard.

⁷We sailed slowly for several days and with great difficulty finally arrived off the town of Cnidus. The wind would not let us go any further in that direction, so we sailed down the sheltered side of the island of Crete, passing by Cape Salmone. ⁸We kept close to the coast and with great difficulty came to a place called Safe Harbours, not far from the town of Lasea.

⁹We spent a long time there, until it became dangerous to continue the voyage, for by now the Day of Atonement was already past. So Paul gave them this advice: ¹⁰"Men, I see that our voyage from here on will be dangerous; there will be great damage to the cargo and to the ship, and loss of life as well." ¹¹But the army officer was convinced by what the captain and the owner of the ship said, and not by what Paul said. ¹²The harbour was not a good one to spend the winter in; so most people were in favour of putting out to sea and trying to reach Phoenix, if possible, in order to spend the winter there. Phoenix is a harbour in Crete that faces south-west and north-west.

The Storm at Sea

¹³A soft wind from the south began to blow, and the men thought that they could carry out their plan, so they pulled up the anchor and sailed as close as possible along the coast of Crete. ¹⁴But soon a very strong wind — the one called "North-easter" — blew down from the island. ¹⁵It hit the ship, and since it was impossible to keep the ship headed into the wind, we gave up trying and let it be carried along by the wind. ¹⁶We got some shelter when we passed to the south of the little island of Cauda. There, with some difficulty, we managed to make the ship's boat secure. ¹⁷They pulled it aboard and then fastened some

ropes tight round the ship. They were afraid that they might run into the sandbanks off the coast of Libya, so they lowered the sail and let the ship be carried by the wind. [18] The violent storm continued, so on the next day they began to throw some of the ship's cargo overboard, [19] and on the following day they threw part of the ship's equipment overboard. [20] For many days we could not see the sun or the stars, and the wind kept on blowing very hard. We finally gave up all hope of being saved.

[21] After those on board had gone a long time without food, Paul stood before them and said, "Men, you should have listened to me and not have sailed from Crete; then we would have avoided all this damage and loss. [22] But now I beg you, take heart! Not one of you will lose your life; only the ship will be lost. [23] For last night an angel of the God to whom I belong and whom I worship came to me [24] and said, 'Don't be afraid, Paul! You must stand before the Emperor. And God in his goodness to you has spared the lives of all those who are sailing with you.' [25] So take heart, men! For I trust in God that it will be just as I was told. [26] But we will be driven ashore on some island."

[27] It was the fourteenth night, and we were being driven about in the Mediterranean by the storm. About midnight the sailors suspected that we were getting close to land. [28] So they dropped a line with a weight tied to it and found that the water was forty metres deep; a little later they did the same and found that it was thirty metres deep. [29] They were afraid that the ship would go on the rocks, so they lowered four anchors from the back of the ship and prayed for daylight. [30] Then the sailors tried to escape from the ship; they lowered the boat into the water and pretended that they were going to put out some anchors from the front of the ship. [31] But Paul said to the army officer and soldiers, "If the sailors don't stay on board, you have no hope of being saved." [32] So the soldiers cut the ropes that held the boat and let it go.

[33] Just before dawn, Paul begged them all to eat some food: "You have been waiting for fourteen days now, and all this time you have not eaten anything. [34] I beg you, then, eat some food; you need it in order to survive. Not even a hair of your heads will be lost." [35] After saying this, Paul took some bread, gave thanks to God before them all, broke it, and began to eat. [36] They took heart, and every one of them also ate some food. [37] There was a total of 276 of us on board. [38] After everyone had eaten enough, they lightened the ship by throwing all the wheat into the sea.

The Shipwreck

[39] When day came, the sailors did not recognize the coast, but they noticed a bay with a beach and decided that, if possible, they would run the ship aground there. [40] So they cut off the anchors and let them sink in the sea, and at the same time they untied the ropes that held the steering oars. Then they raised the sail at the front of the ship so that the wind would blow the ship forward, and we headed for shore. [41] But the ship hit a sandbank and went aground; the front part of the ship got stuck and could not move, while the back part was being broken to pieces by the violence of the waves.

[42] The soldiers made a plan to kill all the prisoners, in order to keep them from swimming ashore and escaping. [43] But the army officer wanted to save Paul, so he stopped them from doing this. Instead, he ordered those who could swim to jump overboard first and swim ashore; [44] the rest were to follow, holding on to the planks or to some broken pieces of the ship. And this was how we all got safely ashore.

In Malta

[1] When we were safely ashore, we learnt that the island was called Malta. [2] The natives there were very friendly to us. It had started to rain and was cold, so they lit a fire and made us all welcome. [3] Paul gathered up a bundle of sticks and was putting them on the fire when a snake came out on account of the heat and fastened itself to his hand. [4] The natives saw the snake hanging on Paul's hand and said to one another, "This man must be a murderer, but Fate will not let him live, even though he escaped from the sea." [5] But Paul shook the snake off into the fire without being harmed at all. [6] They were waiting for him to swell up or suddenly fall down dead. But after waiting for a long time and not seeing anything unusual happening to him, they changed their minds and said, "He is a god!"

[7] Not far from that place were some fields that belonged to Publius, the chief official of the island. He welcomed us kindly and for three days we were his guests. [8] Publius' father was in bed, sick with fever and dysentery. Paul went into his room, prayed, placed his hands on him, and healed him. [9] When this happened, all the other sick people on the island came and were healed. [10] They gave us many gifts, and when we sailed, they put on board what we needed for the voyage.

From Malta to Rome

[11] After three months we sailed away on a ship from Alexandria, called "The Twin Gods", which had spent the winter in the island. [12] We arrived in the city of Syracuse and stayed there for three days. [13] From there we sailed on and arrived in the city of Rhegium. The next day a wind began to blow from the south, and in two days we came to the town of Puteoli. [14] We found some believers there who asked us to stay with them a week. And so we came to Rome. [15] The believers in Rome heard about us and came as far as the towns of Market of Appius and Three Inns to meet us. When Paul saw them, he thanked God and was greatly encouraged.

In Rome

[16] When we arrived in Rome, Paul was allowed to live by himself with a soldier guarding him.

[17] After three days Paul called the local Jewish leaders to a meeting. When they had gathered, he said to them, "My fellow-Israelites, even though I did nothing against our people or the customs that

we received from our ancestors, I was made a prisoner in Jerusalem and handed over to the Romans. [18] After questioning me, the Romans wanted to release me, because they found that I had done nothing for which I deserved to die. [19] But when the Jews opposed this, I was forced to appeal to the Emperor, even though I had no accusation to make against my own people. [20] That is why I asked to see you and talk with you. As a matter of fact, I am bound in chains like this for the sake of him for whom the people of Israel hope."

[21] They said to him, "We have not received any letters from Judea about you, nor have any of our people come from there with any news or anything bad to say about you. [22] But we would like to hear your ideas, because we know that everywhere people speak against this party to which you belong."

[23] So they fixed a date with Paul, and a large number of them came that day to the place where Paul was staying. From morning till night he explained to them his message about the Kingdom of God, and he tried to convince them about Jesus by quoting from the Law of Moses and the writings of the prophets. [24] Some of them were convinced by his words, but others would not believe. [25] So they left, disagreeing among themselves, after Paul had said this one thing: "How well the Holy Spirit spoke through the prophet Isaiah to your ancestors! [26] For he said,

> 'Go and say to this people:
> You will listen and listen, but not understand;
> you will look and look, but not see,
> [27] because this people's minds are dull,
> and they have stopped up their ears
> and closed their eyes.
> Otherwise, their eyes would see,
> their ears would hear,
> their minds would understand,
> and they would turn to me, says God,
> and I would heal them.'"

[28] And Paul concluded: "You are to know, then, that God's message of salvation has been sent to the Gentiles. They will listen!"

[30] For two years Paul lived in a place he rented for himself, and there he welcomed all who came to see him. [31] He preached about the Kingdom of God and taught about the Lord Jesus Christ, speaking with all boldness and freedom.

Glossary

Abraham
Abraham is one of the earliest and most important heroes of the Jewish people. References to Abraham in Luke and Acts are often used to emphasise the continuous growth of God's promise to humanity.

Apostle
A title given to the close followers of Jesus during his life, carrying on his teachings after his death and resurrection. Apostle means 'sent out' in Greek, the language of the New Testament.

Baptise, Baptist
Baptism describes the act of being put in or covered in water as a symbolic ritual for the beginning of a new life with Jesus.

Covenant
An agreement or promise between God and his people.

Gentile
A term to describe anyone who is not originally or culturally Jewish.

Good News
A term to sum up the message of God's activity to rescue humanity, specifically how we are saved through Jesus' death and resurrection, restoring our relationship with God.

Hades
A Greek word used to describe the place or state of human souls upon death. Although often thought of as the same as Hell, Hades actually has two separate and unconnected parts – paradise and hell.

Israel
Originally the name given by God to Jacob, an early leader of the Jewish religion, the word later became used to describe the land promised by God to the Jewish people. In Luke and Acts, Israel is often used to describe the Jewish people as a whole.

Law
The teachings which form the rules of the Jewish religion, principally derived from the first five books of the Jewish Scriptures, the Torah (Genesis, Exodus, Leviticus, Numbers and Deuteronomy). The Torah also forms the basis of the Old Testament.

Messiah
A familiar term in the Jewish religion, it translates as 'anointed one' and is used to describe an individual who will come to lead and save the Jewish people. Some Jews believed that Jesus was the Messiah, and they eventually became the first Christians.

Parable
A simple story used to tell a deeper moral or spiritual meaning or lesson.

Passover
One of the most important Jewish celebrations, commemorating the freeing of the Israelites from slavery in Egypt by Moses. The name comes from the angel of death 'passing over' their houses.

Pharisees
An important religious group within the Jewish faith whose teachings became the foundation of modern-day Judaism.

Prophet
Someone who is inspired by God, through the Holy Spirit, to deliver a message to others.

Repent
Literally meaning 'to turn', it is a word used to describe being sorry for an act of wrongdoing, asking for forgiveness and living differently.

Sabbath
The seventh day of the week, set aside strictly for rest and worship, in the same way that God rested on the seventh day of creation. Many activities were strictly forbidden on the Sabbath.

Sadducees
An important religious group within the Jewish faith during Jesus' time.

Scriptures
The written sacred texts, teachings and laws of the Jewish people, which today make up the Old Testament.

Son of Man
A term used by Jesus to describe himself. Its meaning is not completely clear, but he may have been using it to connect himself directly with prophecies in the Jewish Scriptures.

Synagogue
The Jewish place of worship, where Jews meet for worship and teaching.

More about the Bible

The events you've just read about took place around 2,000 years go, and are recorded in two of the books from the Bible, the Gospel of Luke and The Acts of the Apostles.

The Bible is made up of many books, each with their own style, focus and purpose. Some books are so brief that they're almost like short stories. Some are copies of letters sent to churches and followers of Jesus shortly after his death and resurrection. Others cover events across hundreds of years or bring together proverbs, songs and sayings.

To this day the Bible remains the world's bestselling book. If you don't have a Bible and would like to explore it further, they are available in most bookshops and libraries. If you're interested in buying one, you can get one online at biblesociety.org.uk/shop. Alternatively you can read the Bible online for free by visiting biblesociety.org.uk/explore.

If you are a prisoner, or a migrant or refugee, Bible Society can help you access a copy of the Bible; just speak to one of your chaplains.

When you're reading the Bible, it can be helpful to do the following things:

- Pray: Christians believe that God inspired the Bible; praying when you are reading it helps to tune us into what God might be trying to say to us through its message.

- Be specific: Because the Bible is a collection of books, we don't need to read it from start to finish. Try starting with a letter (or epistle) like Galatians or Ephesians, or reading the grand stories from Genesis or the songs of the Psalms.

- Read with others: Find a Christian to ask questions or share your insights with; attending a church group or service will help you hear the Bible again and again.

- Respond: If there's something that has struck you or inspired you, respond to it in your own life. The Bible challenges us in many ways to be better, to welcome and love others, and to help restore creation. Responding to these challenges can help bring the Bible to life for you and for others and have a profound impact on the world around you.

One way to get into the Bible more is to take part in The Bible Course, an 8-session accessible and interactive small-group course that's designed to enhance and inform your study of the Bible, whether you're new to it or wanting to explore it deeper. More details can be found by visiting biblesociety.org.uk/explore-the-bible/the-bible-course. Alternatively speak to your chaplain, priest or minister.

What next?

To discover more about Jesus, the Bible and the Christian faith, we suggest these three next steps.

- To grow in your faith, a top priority is to meet up with other Christians, by finding a church community or engaging with a chaplaincy group. There are many different types of church out there, so you might want to try a few and see where you feel most comfortable. If you'd like to find out a bit more about the different types of church, you can find out more at christianity.org.uk or speak to a chaplain. You can also visit findachurch.co.uk if you need help finding churches local to you.

- Some churches, Christian communities and chaplaincies run a course called Alpha, designed to cover the basics of Christian faith. It's not for everyone, but it's a good introduction to Christianity and will offer you the chance to meet other Christians and make friends. Visit uk.alpha.org/try or ask a chaplain to find a course for you. Some churches or chaplaincy groups might run similar courses.

- The whole Bible is waiting for you to explore, so get hold of a copy and start reading. Remember, though, that because the Bible is a collection of books, we don't need to read it from start to finish. Try starting with something small, such as a letter (or epistle) like Galatians or Ephesians; go big and read the grand stories of Genesis, or dive into the beauty and emotion of the Psalms. You could even follow a specific Bible reading guide or try to read the whole Bible in a year. Speak to a priest, chaplain or minister and see how your church group is reading the Bible.